THERE IS NOTHING

BUT LOVE
IN GOD

Dec. 2013

Dear Rita,

All God's Love,

Maryanne Lacy

There is Nothing but
Love in God

Maryanne Lacy

Sirena Press

For information:

Murmaid Publishing
Madeira Beach, FL 33738
murmaid@tampabay.rr.com

ISBN  978-0-9819432-4-4

Cover and Book Design
theMurmaid ᵗᵐ
for Sirena Press

Banner Design Rinda Sternberg

Printed in the United States of America

First American Edition

# Dedication

I dedicate this book and my love to
my children, their spouses
and to my grandchildren

Beth, Tom, Alison and James Maschioveccio
Timothy and Elizabeth Lacy
Mary, Pete and Marissa Linkowski
Kathleen Lacy Schaefer and Jessica Lacy
Patrick, Trish and Patrick George Lacy

I am truly grateful from the depths of my heart
for the gift you have been to me.
The memory of each one of you has been
etched on my heart and soul for all eternity.

You remain with me always.

I love you, Mom, (Maura)

# Contents

# Acknowledgements

When I began to write this book I felt very much alone and am now so truly humbled by how each person who helped make this book possible came along just when I needed them. I pray that Our Lord will provide abundant blessings to each and every one who contributed their time in helping me write this book.

First and foremost I am sincerely and deeply grateful to Maura Shaw who was the person who inspired me to write this book. I am always amazed as to how the Holy Spirit connects our lives. Maura came into my life just when I felt I was in a limbo state and she encouraged me by outlining the table of contents of this book. When I had doubts as to whether I would be able to do this she assured me that she would help me when she could. Thank you Maura for your valuable time and caring concern in helping define this manuscript; you were a special gift and blessing in my life.

As soon as my children learned that I was to begin writing this book, they all chipped in and mailed me a brand new Dell computer and so I thank you my dear ones. Special gratitude goes to my son-in-law Tom Maschioveccio who made all the arrangements. Thanks also to Arlene and Guy Kersh, friends and neighbors who came to my assistance in assembling the computer and printer.

I had to learn the computer at the same time I began writing this book and the frustrations of doing that was compounded with not being able to have someone to help me with the complexities of the computer system. However the Holy Spirit saw to it that Chris Maddox, neighbor and friend, was sent just at the time when I needed the help. Thank you Chris, for responding, in spite of your busy work schedule, to the many times I called you for help.

My long time friend and neighbor Rinda Sternberg helped tremendously by doing the tedious work of transcribing some of my audio-cassette tapes into print so that they could be included in this book. I am deeply grateful for her patient work.

Special thanks to Father James Villa, OFM who gave me valuable assistance in providing some biblical clarification. Thanks to my beautiful granddaughter Alison Maschioveccio who gave me some helpful advice and to my friend Kay Stevens who also provided information I needed.

My gratitude goes to all those dear and good friends who gave encouragement by reading through the chapters and providing valuable feedback. They are Sr. Ellie Shea, OSU, Sr. Winifred Danwitz OSU, Ann Babiez, Barbara Beasley Murphy, Kathleen Garvey and Barbara Parrish, Nancy Evans, Shirley Lorenzo and Claudia Hunter, Mary McAuliffe and to my fellow parishioner, Ellen MacRorie. Thanks to neighbor Judy Garrett who also has come to my assistance when I needed it and many blessings to Stephanie Iachetta for contributing helpful ideas to the Chapter on Father Peter McCall.

Jim Gannon was a surprise gift. He had been transcribing Father Peter McCall's audio-cassette tape homilies and putting them into print and offered them to me for this publication. I also extend special thanks to Jim for his heartwarming testimony which can be found at the end of this book.

After most of this manuscript was completed, I printed out a hard copy and sent it to Maura Shaw. I had not realized the importance of a backup system and horror of horrors happened...my computer crashed along with my documents and almost completed manuscript.

Thank God I had run off a hard copy for Maura.

Again I repeat, The Lord is forever good. My dear neighbor Chris Maddox came to the rescue and after many hours of hard work on his part tried to scan the entire manuscript back on my word perfect system. Unfortunately all his efforts were to no avail and the entire manuscript had to be reformatted. Of course I went into prayer and the thought came to me to call another neighbor that I had met at a few social events where I live.

Claudia Hunter had just retired from the school system here in Florida. When I asked her for her help she was more than willing to be of assistance. She has spent countless hours trying to undo the mess-up. What a blessing! With tears in my eyes I thanked the Lord for the goodness that led Claudia to me to help straighten and perfect the manuscript back to its original state. Thank you Claudia! I give glory to God now and forever!

I would like to thank the Gulf Beaches Library writing group for their valuable critique.

My deepest gratitude goes to the following:

Gerry and Lou Gerenscer, Rinda Sternberg, Isabel Milano, Sandy Edmonson, and Dr. Alfred J. Modica for their generous support in helping me publish this book.

## Introduction

I was a Sunday church going Catholic all my life, but had not yet experienced the joy of knowing an unconditionally loving Creator.

That all changed when after a period of depression –a dark night of the soul– I felt an inner calling to a deeper spiritual life.

In 1973 I experienced a spiritual awakening, a profound awareness of a divine light and Loving Presence that ultimately changed my life. This revealed to me that I had a gift that was being awakened in order to bring healing and help to those who were in the bondage of depression as well as suffering from other various infirmities.

I continue this healing work, to bring enlightenment to those who want it spiritually, emotionally and physically.

I was introduced to Father Peter McCall, a Franciscan priest, in 1978, who had the same calling. Together we cofounded a Prayer Center, The House of Peace Inc., in New York. We did the work of healing and touching countless numbers of people through the years and co-authored three books on healing prayer and many audio-cassette tapes of meditations and affirmations.

Forty Eight Hours, The Learning Channel, CNN, and Headline News featured us and our ministry during healing services at various churches.

Sadly, Father Peter died suddenly without warning in the spring of 2001. The House of Peace healing prayer ministry closed following his death. We were the longest running healing ministry in the Diocese of New York at the time of his passing.

I remain deeply committed to contemplative prayer and meditation which offer a way to promote healing in our lives as we begin to open up to this loving Presence.

The power of affirmation is a tool to help undo negative memory patterns. The exercises outlined offer hopeful ways to begin the process of healing the wounds that this life produces.

I feel the calling to share what I have experienced and learned throughout these many years; a passion to teach others how to trust in an unconditionally loving Creator. God's overflowing love and joy can be experienced by all who are searching for the fullness of life in the here and now.

Although this book is rooted in the Roman Catholic tradition, the messages it contains can be shared with a wider audience. Passages from the Old and New Testaments can inspire new prayers that illuminate the presence of the Divine in our lives.

I pray you will be irresistibly drawn to the heart of Jesus, the Christ, through reading this book. I pray for those seeking to be restored in body, mind and spirit, that you will find inner joy, love and peace. May forgiveness become a way of life in helping you to maintain a state of harmony and balance.

*"Rejoice in the Lord always! I say it again. Rejoice! Everyone should see how unselfish you are. The Lord is near. Dismiss all anxiety from your minds. Present your needs to God in every form of prayer and in petitions full of gratitude. Then God's own peace which is beyond all understanding will stand guard over your hearts and minds, in Christ Jesus." (Phil. 4:4-8).*

# Chapter 1

"Peace is My Gift to You!"

Learning to trust in the Lord.

*"On the Evening of that first day of the week, even though the disciples had locked the doors of the place where they were for fear of the Jews, Jesus came and stood before them. 'Peace be with you,' He said. When he had said this, he showed them his hands and his side. At the sight of the Lord the disciples rejoiced. 'Peace be with you,' He said again. 'As the Father has sent me so I send you.' Then he breathed on them and said: 'Receive the Holy Spirit.'" (Jn. 20:19-22)*

With an amazing grace and a miracle of salvation I was able to come to believe that there is nothing but love in God. There was a time when I was absolutely terrified of God. The first person of the Trinity known as God the Father had me recoiling in dread and fear, for I believed "He" was not to be trusted and wanted to punish us for any little infraction we might commit.

Most of my life I was plagued by depression and anxiety; however I did not realize it. It was just the way I perceived life. Usually I was able to mask my feelings with cheerfulness and a smile because there was no sense in looking glum, certainly not in the family I grew up in.

At the age of eleven I believed that life was a drudge, everything looked dark. We had just moved from a country setting in the Riverdale section of The Bronx, down to the hard pavement of the West Side of Manhattan to a five story Brownstone walk-up.

No one in the family noticed my loss of appetite and how sad I had become. My father observed how thin I was and suggested a daily dose of eggnog. He showed me how to make it with vanilla extract and milk, as if that would cure whatever was ailing me.

In spite of my mental state I managed to graduate from Catholic grammar school with excellent grades and high school with honors. I became engaged to two different boys, married one and had two children, all this between the years 1950 to 1959.

The '60s brought three more children and by '69 I began having trouble sleeping because of anxieties. I had five young children and an unhappy marriage. I had to keep the windows in the bedroom open at night, even in freezing temperatures, for I felt as if I were suffocating.

The world was a bleak place and my anxieties eventually accelerated to panic attacks. I fell on my knees in despair and asked the Lord to help me. I sought professional help and with medication and counseling I managed to survive that time.

After Vatican Council II, (1962–65) Catholics were encouraged to read the bible. A friend urged me to join a neighborhood bible study group; I looked forward to this glimmer of light.

One night after tossing restlessly, I went out to the living room and randomly opened my brand new bible. It opened to the gospel of Matthew. "Which of you by worrying can add a moment to his life-span? As for clothes, why be concerned? Learn a lesson from the way the wild flowers grow. They do not work; they do not spin. Yet I assure you, not even Solomon in all his splendor was arrayed like one of these. If God can clothe in such splendor the grass of the field, which blooms today and is thrown on the fire tomorrow, will he not provide much more for you, O weak in faith! Stop worrying, then, over questions like what are we to eat, or what are we to drink, or what are we to wear? The unbelievers are always running after these things. Your Heavenly Father knows all that you need. Seek first his kingship over you, his way of holiness and all of these things will be given you as well." (6:27-34)

Closing the bible that night I felt so uplifted and joyful, I sincerely believed that Jesus was speaking to me personally. I was desperate for help, overwhelmed with anxieties. These particular words of scripture burned into my soul and spoke to my need for inner peace.

After this my night terrors ceased to plague me. It began to dawn on me that just maybe God was concerned about me personally. Perhaps I should trust in the Lord for the help I needed. I sincerely wanted to follow God's will and began prayerfully, with some trepidation, to seek that course for my life.

Although I had a long way to go before I could say I was freed from having depressed periods, there was hope; an awakening that The Light was not far away. I wanted so much more and so snatched at the mysterious spiritual dimension that drew me, like a magnet, to a power far greater than I ever knew existed before.

Prayer for the healing of depression:
O most wondrous and loving Lord God, I need your help. Everything looks so bleak and dark to me. I am so sick of being so sick. The sadness I feel is impacting every aspect of my life. I am obsessed with sorrows and regrets. There have been too many losses in my life. I want to be happy again. Please show me how. My fears and anxieties paralyze me

from living life. I am in sheer terror and have no peace. I
often have thoughts of leaving this world. I know I need your
help and your grace. You are the only one I can turn to.
Everything I have tried has failed me. Deliver me from this
darkness. You know me and know what I need. I yearn for
inner peace and for the gift of joy. Joy eludes me night and
day. You are the healer of my soul. Set me free O Lord God
that I may see the light of your love for me. Blessed be your
holy name now and forever. Amen.

The Catholic Church was experiencing a new phenom-
enon in the movement of the Charismatic Renewal.

In 1967 the first group of Pentecostal Catholics experienced the gifts of the Holy Spirit in the manner that
had been recorded in the Acts of the Apostles.

Students and faculty from two Catholic universities,
Duquesne in Pittsburg and later the University of Notre
Dame in Indiana reasoned that the early church had
encountered the fullness of the Holy Spirit and so went
on a retreat to pray for the "Baptism of the Holy Spirit."

They believed that "God's Action" was alive and well
and must be prepared for prayerfully by reading the
Acts of the Apostles and other accounts of experiences
of the Holy Spirit.

What happened as a result spread quickly throughout Catholic and non-Catholic believers throughout this
country and eventually countries throughout the world.
I first heard about it in 1972 from friends in our parish
church and attended my first charismatic experience in
Fordham University, Bronx, New York.

In charismatic style of prayer, people are free to
raise their hands during hymns of praise. This form of
worship is characterized by vibrant Masses as well as
prayer meetings where people might prophesy and pray
in tongues, and manifest the gift of healing through the

laying on of hands.

Christians generally believe all this existed in the early church as described in the Bible and should still be practiced today. This is what I saw when I attended my first Catholic charismatic Mass. Three hundred believers met each week at the chapel for Mass with prayerful and lively music leading us in praise and worship. My thirst for the spiritual was being quenched that first night.

I attended a seven week seminar to learn more about the Holy Spirit and the surrendering of oneself to the Lordship of Jesus Christ in all parts of life. The last week of the seminar was for us to experience the "Baptism of the Holy Spirit" through the laying on of hands. There were one hundred eager participants and on the last night we broke up into groups of ten with our group leaders.

One by one each of us were prayed over while invoking the Holy Spirit to release within us all the gifts and graces we were given at our baptism and confirmation. It was one of the holiest evenings of my life up to that point.

I was the very last in my group to be prayed with, not knowing what to expect. When hands were laid upon me I felt an immediate warmth flow throughout my body. I became engulfed in a light that overtook all my senses. It was touching my inner being with a love unknown before and beyond what this world could ever offer.

I was so overcome by the encounter I began weeping from the bottom of my soul. I was surrounded by the supportive arms of my spiritual companions and embraced with loving concern. I cried and cried that night like I had never cried before but these were cleansing tears of joy and comfort, of knowing finally that I was truly loved. Loved by the person of Jesus the Christ, the one I had been taught about all my life but had never experienced the reality of his existence until now. I fell passionately in love with The Lord that night and I have never been the same since.

> Let us pray:
> Lord, I choose to release all my cares and worries to you this day, all my past and present anxieties. I desire to place my trust in your love for me as I invite the Holy Spirit to heal me at the core of my being. I thank you for your comfort and consolations as I learn to relax and rest in your caring concern for me.
> I affirm and acknowledge that you God are helping me to overcome all my fears. I am truly grateful for your love. Amen.

Joyful Confidence in God:
*"O Lord, let the light of your countenance shine upon us! You put gladness into my heart, more than when grain and wine abound. As soon as I lie down, I fall peacefully asleep, for you alone O Lord, bring security to my dwelling." (Psalm 4:8-9)*

As I continued my spiritual journey and my quest for inner peace, I attended charismatic prayer meetings regularly. Eventually I was led to go on a retreat where the priest introduced us to Inner Healing prayer. This retreat enlightened me about the need for continued inner healing and to realize that this was what my soul was yearning for.

## What Is Inner Healing?
"Inner healing, healing of memories and healing the child within" are all part and parcel of the same thing.

The past is as gone as this morning's breakfast or

yesterday's news.

The past holds us in memory only. Memories can be good, bad or neutral. Unfortunately we tend to bring negative memories into the present and also project them into the future. Unhealed memories continue to be a problem if we make the same mistakes in the present that we made in the past.

I know more than one woman who has divorced an alcoholic husband only to marry another, divorce that one, and still marry another. Memories continue to have a negative power over us in the here and now as we hold on to grievances and unforgiveness of people who we believe have hurt us.

In order to mature healthily in mind and spirit, we need to recognize that we are in need of inner healing. Denial is a powerful defense mechanism. Our need is to learn how to forgive and love again. Life offers us challenges in learning how to forgive—and this life requires constant forgiveness. Jesus tells us we need to forgive over and over and over again. (Re: Luke 17:3) If we learn our lessons well, forgiveness becomes a way of life, not only in forgiving others, but ourselves as well.

This is not easy without the help of the Holy Spirit. The Holy Spirit is our Helper, our Advocate, our source of comfort and consolation and is the working power behind our need and our desire to be released from our hoarded hurts and grievances. I have participated in the healing of my own life's hurts for well over thirty-five years now and still have to work to forgive myself and others for what I have perceived to be past errors.

Let us pray:
Loving Lord God, Pour out your Holy Spirit upon me and in me for I am in need of much help in order that I may receive the willingness to forgive myself and others. I tend to be

stubborn 0 Lord and I resist my own good and fail to see the goodness in others. Help me now to give and receive forgiveness that I may be cleansed from the hurtful memories that keep me bound in this present moment. Heal me of childhood wounds by the power of your love. I thank you as I go forward in quiet expectation knowing you are in the process of loving and purifying me. Amen.

## In The Quiet

In my childhood there was very little peace. I recall a noisy and violent home life. In my adulthood I was the mother of five precocious children and did not set boundaries. Our home was open to all my friends and those of my husband and children, including my in-laws and family. Anyone could walk in at any time. The world I lived in was inundated with noise. I used to feel so confused and would seek out a peaceful place wherever I could find it, and that was usually after the children were old enough to go to school.

After my spiritual awakening I found I needed quiet time to pray and reflect. I had heard through spiritual teachers that it was in the quiet that God speaks to us. Learning to quiet my mind through practice and discipline was not an easy task. In the beginning I did not hear an audible voice. I knew that some prayerful people did hear the voice of the Holy Spirit but it took me a while of learning to quiet my mind, my inner self, before I could reach that stage. Although it was not easy I was inspired by the story of Elijah from the Book of Kings in the Old Testament. It is a story that is worth contemplating for it is a lesson on how to listen for God's voice in the quiet.

## The Story Of Elijah

"Elijah was a great prophet in Israel and was escaping from Jezebel, the wife of Ahab, the king of Israel. It was the first time that a king of Israel had allied himself by marriage with a heathen princess. Elijah had managed to infuriate her by putting her idolatry to the test and then slaying her false prophets. And so Jezebel was determined to destroy him.

"Elijah fled to the desert. There he prayed to die, but an angel came to him with food and water beckoning Elijah to continue his journey. Eventually he came to a cave and was given instructions to wait, for 'the Lord would be passing by.' A strong and heavy wind was rending the mountains and crushing rocks before the Lord...but the Lord was not in the wind. After the wind there was an earthquake...but the Lord was not in the earthquake. After the earthquake there was a fire...but the Lord was not in the fire.

"*After the fire there was a tiny whispering sound. When he heard this, Elijah hid his face in his cloak and went and stood at the entrance of the cave.*" (1 Kings 19: 9-13)

It was in this still, quiet whispering sound that Elijah was able to hear what the Lord wanted to say to him and thus give him a solution to his problem.

It is important to know that in the Hebrew Scriptures, hyperbole and exaggeration are used in order to get a point across. It is so common in Biblical writings and yet so frequently overlooked. A very simple device, it very clearly shows that the Biblical authors assumed an audience and that the Bible text cannot properly be understood without taking this fact into account.

Before written Scripture there was an oral tradition of telling stories and using exaggeration as a form of emphasis. The major issue in the story of Elijah is the nature of divine revelation. God is revealed by means of the word, here the spoken word and not fundamentally through the manipulation of natural forces. That word is calm, comprehensible, personal and purposeful.

There are other ways of hearing the Lord. Sometimes it is with an intuition, a prompting, a nudge or through someone else's spoken word. It can be through nature, or even a bumper sticker on the back of someone's automobile. The Holy Spirit is quite creative in ways to help us to listen.

> Let us pray:
> Loving Lord God, teach us, show us how to avoid worrying about the past or fearing the future .Teach us how to live in the present moment. Help us to learn to be silent, so as to be aware of Your Loving Presence within and around us. As we turn within to the quiet within our souls, teach us your ways, 0 Lord, for we want to know you and to love you. We come before you in sincerity and humility realizing our need of your gentle kindness and loving attention. Blessed be the holy name of Our Lord and Savior, Jesus Christ. Amen.

## Contemplative Prayer

Contemplative prayer is a process of entering into the silence within. The early fathers of the church went into the desert in order to leave the distractions of the world. They sought after solitude so as to be able to listen and reflect on the word of God. In time they developed methods to help those of us who were not called to a monastery but who desire to have a deeper walk with God in our daily lives.

One of the methods these holy men formulated is called Centering Prayer. The term was originally coined by Thomas Merton, the Trappist Monk whose story is written in his autobiography, "Seven Story Mountain."

In Centering Prayer there are certain guidelines and instructions that are helpful. Centering prayer requires discipline. It is a simple form of prayer but not easy to achieve. The only requirement is that we desire to be aware of God's presence and so we consent to that Divine presence by practicing this prayer on a daily basis.

I believe that we are divinely inspired and called to this type of prayer at a time when the soul wants to advance in the spiritual journey. I had tried many different types of meditation and contemplation until after many years I finally found myself drawn by the Spirit to this particular form. The guidelines are as follows:

Choose a sacred word, preferably with one or two syllables as a symbol of your intention to consent to God's presence and action within. Some ideas for a sacred word could be: Lord, Abba, Love, Peace, Mother Mary, etc. Choose one for yourself that will not be a distraction.

Sitting comfortably with eyes closed settle briefly, and silently introduce the sacred word as the symbol of your consent to God's presence and action within.

When you start to become aware of thoughts, return gently to the sacred word. See your thoughts as moving along a stream of water. Let them pass by, and return again and again ever so gently to your sacred word.

In the beginning it has been suggested that the minimum span of time for this prayer period should be twenty minutes.

If you practice this on your own you may want to use a timer to remind you when twenty minutes are up, preferably a soft sounding one so as not to create a startled response.

At the end of the prayer time, remain quiet for a few minutes and gently open your eyes, becoming aware of your surroundings. Saying the Our Father at this time could be a way of ending the prayer time.

I prefer to say a short prayer before beginning, for example: "0 Lord come to my assistance, 0 God make haste to help me."

Centering Prayer is not meant to replace other forms of prayer but can be helpful in our becoming more conscious of how God is leading us in the healing process.

Let us pray:
Loving Lord God grant me the grace I need to continue the path of prayer that leads to an ongoing relationship with you. I am in need of much healing especially for peace of mind. I thank you that my thoughts are being transformed and that you are renewing my mind. Thank you for your loving presence in my life. Thank you for a new awareness of your life within me that is awakening me to the truth of who I really am...your beloved child. Amen and Amen.

## The Healing Of Memories Prayer

The Healing of Memories prayer is based on the New Testament passages: *"Jesus Christ is the same yesterday, today and forever." (Hebrews 13:8)* and "With *the Lord one day is like a thousand years, and a thousand years is like one day." (2 Peter 3:8).* In other words in the Kingdom of God there is no time or space. Time is an earthly invention and so God is only in this present moment by moment experience.

Unhealthy experiences in the past can linger in our memories and be reactivated by events in the present. As long as a memory has not been healed, it can continue to haunt us in the present. Most phobias can be traced to this root cause.

We cannot change what historically happened to us but we can change the power it has over us. Past memories such as the loss of a loved one by abandonment, accident or death, can be extremely painful. There is no way we can be free of the pain unless we are willing to be helped. Other painful past memories probably include childhood traumas and abuses of every kind. What would be impossible for us to do alone, we can do by trusting the Lord as our guide.

How can we do this you may ask? An event in the past has negative power over us because of our unhealed interpretation of it. Today, we see only our version of what happened in the past, not the past event itself.

For example, I have five children and have observed that when they are discussing something that happened in their childhood they all have different memories of it. They each have their own perception of what occurred. This is true of most people. What needs to be healed is not so much the historical event, but our perception of it. Here is where the Divine Presence, our Higher Power, or the Christ Light comes in. It will be the role of the Holy Spirit's loving intervention, helping us to interpret the past event that will eventually heal us.

It has been my experience that not everyone is open to the Healing of Memories prayer perhaps because they are unwilling to bring past memories deliberately to mind. It has helped me tremendously, however, and Lord knows I desperately wanted to be set free from every negative thought that prevented me from living life to the fullest. Jesus tells us: *"I came that you might have life and have it to the full." (Jn. 10:10).*

The Healing of Memories prayer requires that we be open to being healed of painful memories that keep us bound to the past. These are memories that keep us fearful and prevent us from becoming free spiritually, emotionally, and physically in the here and now. The Healing of Memories prayer can defuse the power that the negativity of the past maintains over us to prevent us from becoming more fully alive, healthy human beings in the present.

This form of prayer is helpful for people who suffer

from Post Traumatic Stress Disorder (PTSD). The term PTSD was coined as a result of the Vietnam War veteran's experience. It is a disorder that can occur following the experience or witnessing of life-threatening events such as military combat, natural disasters, terrorist incidents, serious accidents, or violent personal assaults like rape or living in a violent family system.

People who suffer PTSD often relive the experience through nightmares and flashbacks, have difficulty sleeping and feel detached or estranged. These symptoms can be severe enough and last long enough to significantly impair the person's daily life. According to the United States Department of Veterans Affairs, a national study of American civilians conducted in 2005 reports that PTSD occurs in about eight percent of all Americans.

The Healing of Memories prayer can work in conjunction with whatever forms of medical treatment the person decides upon. It is better to have someone you trust such as a spiritual director or prayer counselor to guide you in this prayer. I highly recommend this, especially for the beginner. However you can do this on your own if you have been used to practicing contemplative prayer.

It is important to choose a place you call your quiet space, a sacred place where you feel safe and protected from outside interferences. Perhaps you need to develop a space for yourself. This is essential if you desire a deeper prayer life. Try to do this at a time when you will not be interrupted by anyone. Take your time to quiet down and be still. *"Be still and know that I am God."* *(Psalm 46:10)*

If you are a beginner, it will take some time and practice to do this. (There are many books on meditation that may help you practice in becoming quiet).

Let us pray:
Loving Lord God, it is in quiet and stillness that we are able
to hear you speaking to us. We want to take this time to be
in your loving presence so that we might be able to hear
your gentle voice instructing us. Teach us 0 Lord to quiet
ourselves ever so gently so that we may be able to enter into
a peaceful space, the place where you dwell within us. Help
us to enter into the kingdom within where only love, joy and
wisdom abides. We desire to be at peace and we desire to
be one with you so that we can be in accord with your holy
will. Never let us be separated from you for only in you can
be found our true love. You are that one true love, that one
true voice that will lead us to the heavenly realms where
we belong. We thank you and bless you, now and forever.
Amen.

Take time to invite the Presence of the God of your understanding into your awareness. You may picture this
Presence as light or any other image that appeals to you.
Whatever image you use, know that this Loving Presence understands what you are going through. Our loving God does not deny what you are feeling or tell you
how you ought to feel.

Think of a particular person, event, or situation that
brings up negative emotions such as anger, guilt, depression, or sadness. Look at this memory and feel all
the hurt the memory brings up. Do not deny your feelings. Feelings are neither good nor bad, they are just
feelings. Now bring your image of God into your memory. Practicing the Presence of God in any particular
memory softens the impact of the negativity and can
defuse the power the memory has over us in the present
and future.

The reason why this particular memory makes you
feel so hurt is because you probably believed you were

all alone at the time of the experience. But in the now moment, God is with you. Your awareness of the Divine Presence is essential. This process is not to deny what happened but to realize in this present moment you are being given Divine assistance.

Take your time. There is no need to hurry with this process. The Lord will lead you in proportion to your ability and willingness to see differently. This process will be unique and quite personal. No two people will do this exactly the same way. There is no right or wrong way to do it. The Lord will tailor your healing according to your personal needs.

What is important is that you realize there are no requirements to doing this inner work. The change will come about in accord with your willingness to surrender the memory and to be healed by an unconditionally loving and caring Creator. The healing will be done for you. All that is asked of you is your willingness to accept the shift of perception. When you are ready you will accept it.

*"Alleluia. I will give thanks to the Lord with all my heart in the company and assembly of the just. Great are the works of the Lord, exquisite in all their delights. Majesty and glory are his work, and his justice endures forever. He has renown for his wondrous deeds; gracious and merciful is the Lord." (Psalm 111:1-4)*

## Forgiveness

Forgiveness will be a major part of the Healing of Memories prayer. It is important to remember that we can try to forgive too soon. We may have to work through feelings of anger and rage for some time before we can begin to do the work of forgiveness. The Lord will wait and so should you.

You may feel led to seek the help of a professional or share your experiences with a mature spiritual person such as a spiritual director or sponsor. It is wise to follow your best instincts. Whatever the outcome, you have made progress toward healing just by your willingness to enter into this process. It is important for you to know that our unconditionally loving God wants our past memories healed so that we can be at peace in the present.

## A Personal Experience

The following story illustrates how a Healing of Memories prayer worked for me.

When I was a child of about seven, I received a small second-hand bicycle from someone. We were, during those years, by no means well off. The bicycle was in need of repair and my father promised to fix it for me so I could use it. Time went by and the bicycle still lay in the basement. One day as the children on our block refused me a ride on their bicycles, I decided to take matters into my own hands. I had discovered that my stepmother had a great deal of power over my father. All she had to do was ask for something and it was done. I tried to use this power at my young and impressionable age.

My father was at his workbench in the basement, so I approached him just before dinner time. I told him that my stepmother sent me to ask him to fix the bicycle. In truth, she had sent me to fetch him to dinner. Well, when the deception was uncovered about a half-hour later, that was the end of the bicycle then and forever.

It remained in the basement, unfixed, and I never knew what became of it. The impact of this experience always made me feel as though asking for anything might result in dire consequences. Oftentimes I held back from asking for help when I needed it and tried to work it out by myself. It often left me with feelings of helplessness and frustration.

Some thirty years later I was introduced to a Healing of Memories Seminar led by Ruth Carter Stapleton, the sister of President Jimmy Carter. In the early 1970s it was unusual in Catholic circles to attend something like this. Our prayer group was curious enough to find out what it was all about, and so we went to the Wainwright House in Rye, New York, sometime in the mid 1970s. This was before Jimmy Carter became president and before Ruth herself had become quite famous as a spiritual healer.

We were in for a surprise, as we had never seen a spiritual healer before. We were unprepared to see someone who looked more like a movie actress. Ruth was young, blonde, vivacious, extremely gracious, and very pretty. She wore a long evening dress, looking quite lovely she spoke with a soft Southern drawl. Ruth was convincing when she shared that she believed Jesus could and would heal any memory in our lives, as Scripture was very clear: *"Jesus Christ is the same yesterday, today and forever." (Hebrews 13:8).*

That night she led us in an introduction to a Healing of Memories prayer. It opened up a wonderful new dimension of healing for many of us who were new to the workings of the Holy Spirit during the early days of the charismatic renewal in the Christian Churches. This medium of prayer eventually became a standard in the Inner Healing process. But at that time it was all very new to everyone, as was the charismatic renewal in the mainstream churches.

About a year later, I attended a Catholic healing retreat and the priest who was directing the retreat led us in a Healing of Memories prayer. As I closed my eyes and entered into the prayer, seemingly out of nowhere, I remembered the poor bicycle of my childhood. All the embarrassment, disappointment, guilt, and sadness surfaced and I thought, "Wow, I haven't thought about that in a very long time." Then just as suddenly as these emotions and the memory surfaced, there appeared an image in my mind's eye.

Much to my wonderment appeared Jesus on a two-wheeler bicycle, beckoning me to hop on the back. I went with it, observing Jesus with hair and white robe trailing in the breeze while we went flying down this steep road. I held on tightly. The part of me that was observing this scene was taken up with the incredible joy that was exuding from Jesus. He and the little seven-year-old Maryanne were having the ride of their lives. I can still remember every aspect of it vividly to this day.

The joy of that experience cancelled out the negative emotions of that painful memory. The scene with Jesus had overtaken the other sad scene in the basement.

This healing amazed me and awakened in me a keen awareness of what God was about in my life. The past does not have to have the power over us to keep us in pain. I was learning there was a loving God, and that this loving God cares about me intimately and personally.

What an awesome revelation! Deeply grateful for the new opening in my soul I was becoming more aware, day by day, minute by minute, or all at once of being loved by this healing Presence.


Let us pray:
0 Loving Lord God you are the restorer of my life. Amen.


A Prayer For The Healing Of Memories
*Jesus Christ is the same yesterday, today and forever."*
*(Heb. 13:8).*

Let us pray:

Loving Jesus, we hold the scripture in mind...that you are truly present in this moment because you are the same yesterday, today and forever. We offer you all our memories, our fears, and our unhealed unconscious mind. You know all things and so you know when a particular memory is ready to be healed. Your knowledge is beyond our understanding. We ask to be made ready, to be prepared to break away from our denials and defenses in order to surrender our memories to you for healing. Bring our dark memories into the light of your truth and love. Set us free from the blocks to the awareness of your unconditional love. We sometimes find it difficult to believe, dear Jesus. To believe you can be in the here and now, in this present moment healing us of the dark memories of our past. Life has created deep wounds in our heart and spirit to the point where faith requires a great deal of effort and will on our part 0 Lord, help us in removing our doubts so that we may trust you more. Rekindle in us the memory that lies imbedded in our souls, within the core of our minds, that is, the memory of our Creator God, loving us into life. Lord Jesus, we place our memories under your guidance, for you are the Savior of every moment of our existence. We release our sorrows and our despair into the light of your healing Presence. We let go of any negative memories that would keep us back from experiencing your sweet, sweet Love. We place our lives in your tender and loving care. Amen.

I often led the congregation in the Healing of Memories prayer after Holy Communion during a Healing Mass. This is a sacred time reminding us in the present moment of communion that we are not separated from God. The Spirit of God is within and coupled with this sacred experience of awareness, we can be in an inner communion with the Divine. This is Ultimate Reality. The present moment is where we experience God's perfect and unconditional love.

When I enter the experience of contemplative prayer I gradually become aware that I am not alone. During my quiet time in the early hours of the morning and in the silence of the evening, I center myself using a sacred word to keep the focus on the reason why I am doing this. I am here to remember I am one with God.

When painful memories from the past arise I turn them over to this loving Presence. This is a process in centering prayer that is called unloading. The unloading of the unconscious releases and frees us from painful memories. We no longer need to remember in a painful way, nor do we have to remain victims of the past. In this present moment we are freed at last.

## The Kingdom of God is Within

When we embark on a healing journey and embrace contemplative prayer or meditation as part of our daily routine, we will rarely feel alone again. This requires faithfulness in practicing the Presence and eventually becomes a way of life. The present moment is indeed just that—a wonderful present.

To live in the present moment is what some may call mindfulness. To live in the present moment is to become aware, to become awakened to the Kingdom of God within. This was a favorite theme of Jesus. *"Once, having been asked by the Pharisees when the Kingdom of God would come, Jesus replied, 'The Kingdom of God does not come with your careful observation, nor will people say, 'here it is,' or 'there it is,' because the Kingdom of God is within you." (Luke 17:20-21)*

The work of healing is about the manifestation of the "Kingdom of God." The miracles of healing for Jesus involved more than those being healed. The miracles were a proclamation of the Kingdom of God alive and well in this world. Healing is entering more deeply into the Kingdom of God. Healing prayer is nothing else but asking for the Kingdom of God to rule over our minds and bodies.

Healing prayer is getting in touch with the Kingdom of God within, so that our will and God's will are the same. The Kingdom of God is inevitable. The parable of the Sower and the Seed illustrates this. (Mt. 13:4-23).

Most of Chapter 13 in the Gospel of Matthew addresses parables of Jesus and the reign of God. In verses 31-32, the Parable of the Mustard Seed he proposed still another parable. "The reign of God is like a mustard seed which someone took and sowed in his field. It is the smallest seed of all, yet when full grown it is the largest of plants." Parables of the Yeast, the Treasure and the Pearl and the Parable of the Net all direct the reader to understand how the Kingdom of God comes about in our lives. It will happen with or without our consent. Our resistance can only delay it.

Our participation in the Kingdom of God is our "response-ability," that is, our personal response to an invitation to a Kingdom already here and now. In learning the practice of this we are in fact entering into the Kingdom wherein we rest in this Divine Presence. It is in this Presence that we will experience serenity in the "Peace that passes all Understanding." This gentle Presence will carry us back into conscious union with the God of unlimited life and love.

Let us pray:
Loving Lord God we come before you in humble supplication. We ask for your grace to be poured out upon us. We desire the peace that passes all understanding. All we need is within us for the Kingdom of Heaven awaits us there. Help us to understand that our function is to rest in you and you

alone. When we rest and relax in you, then your Glory can shine through us. It is your Life within us that helps us to be peaceful and quiet. We are in your Loving Presence where we have longed to be from the moment of our existence. We praise and thank you now and forever. We pray that the obstacles to the awareness of your grace and love will be removed ever so gently as we learn to trust you in this present moment. Heal us of our false perceptions. Heal our minds so we may know the truth of your wondrous love and your everlasting goodness.... your glorious light. We thank you and praise your holy name now and forever. Amen!

This awareness of God's love overwhelms me and I want to join with the psalmist in proclaiming the glory of God's wondrous and beautiful nature.

## The Greatness and Goodness of God

*"I will extol you, O my God and King,*
*And I will bless your name forever and ever.*
*Every day will I bless you, and I will praise your*
*name forever and ever.*

*Great is the Lord and highly to be praised: His*
*greatness is unsearchable. Generation after gen-*
*eration praises your works and proclaims your*
*might.*

*They speak of the splendor of your glorious Majesty*
*and tell of your wondrous works, the discourse of*
*the power of your amazing deeds and declare your*
*greatness. They publish the fame of your abundant*
*goodness and joyfully sing of your justice." (Psalm*
*145:1-7)*

# Chapter 2

God's Gift of Healing

The Practice of a Healing Prayer Ministry

## In Praise of Divine Goodness

*"Bless the Lord, 0 my Soul; and all my being bless his holy name. Bless the Lord 0 my soul, and forget not all his Benefits; He pardons all your iniquities; he heals all your ills. He redeems your life from destruction, he crowns your life with kindness and compassion, He fills your lifetime with Good; your youth is renewed like the eagles." (Psalm 103:1-5)*

In the spring of 1976, God chose to begin a new chapter in my life. It was a cold, stormy March night in New York, with strong winds and sheets of pouring rain. It was the night of our weekly prayer group. I decided to stay home, not wanting to go out of the comfort of my home and drive in that kind of weather.

However, I began to feel unsettled about my decision. I didn't understand why, but I had no peace, and felt a nagging within me to go anyway. I can't really say

I prayed about the decision at the time; I just felt uneasy and my mind and heart were drawn to make the trip to the prayer meeting. I decided to chance it and go. Once I made the decision I felt an urgency to get there.

Driving there was difficult, yet I felt it was not me who was driving, but that I was being driven. I arrived at the home of my friends, the couple who led the prayer group. No one else came that night, except a woman who was in a great deal of distress. She explained to us that she came in desperation because she had an obstruction in her throat and the doctors wanted to operate and remove it. She coughed a great deal and expressed hope that through our prayers she would not have to undergo the surgery.

My self-esteem in those days shifted up, and then down; an emotional roller-coaster ride. I now see the wisdom behind my being pushed into going that night. Feelings of self-doubt and lack of self-confidence had dominated me and I usually kept my distance, choosing to stay in the background.

A prayer meeting usually consisted of singing hymns of praise and worship, bible reading and sharing. After, it was the custom to pray with members who requested it through the laying on of hands. I was my usual reticent self that night and expected my friends to take the reins and lead the prayers, and I would stand back and support them.

However, this night there were only four of us instead of the usual twelve or more people. This woman had come expecting us to help her and she was relying on the three of us to pray for a healing to remove the obstruction in her throat. As we began to offer up prayers, the woman sat in a chair with me standing behind her and the other two on each side as they placed a hand on each shoulder.

I placed both my hands on top of her head and closed

my eyes. As we joined together in prayer, I began to experience an all-engulfing gentle Presence. It immersed and bathed me in warmth. I began to be aware of a glowing atmosphere. I recall being lifted up softly into another realm of a heavenly nature where there was only love and peace. I felt light as a feather.

As I allowed myself to flow with the experience I felt a loving Presence and was completely taken over by it. Without any effort or power of my own, I felt my hands lift from this woman's head and ever so gently touch her throat. In a voice, spoken through me, came the words, "Heavenly Father, in the name of Jesus your son, and through the power of the Holy Spirit, I ask that this obstruction be removed from this woman's throat."

A few moments of silence passed, then she declared in surprise and awe that she had felt the growth disappear. She looked up at me and said, "When this young lady, placed her hands on my throat I felt it go away."

We were astonished but delighted and amazed at the same time. It was confirmed later by her doctor that indeed the growth in her throat had vanished. This was how God's new set of plans for me began. *"0 Lord, my God, I cried out to you and you healed me." (Psalm 30:3)*

Let us pray:
0 Lord, you are my strength and comfort in my time of need. I thank you for your calming presence when I need assurance that you are with me. You know me better than I know myself and I am thankful that you lovingly and gently encourage me whenever I am in doubt. I turn to you 0 loving Lord when I am fearful and anxious. Knowing you are with me soothes and comforts me. You are my life, my hope, my freedom. Thank you for revealing your sweet love to me. Thank you for the gift of your healing power. Yours is a power that restores and recreates and brings life and health. Help me to understand that there is great power in the words I speak. Help me to express healing words that will bless

and encourage. O Lord, you are the answer to every need of body, mind and spirit. I will praise your name now and forever. Blessed be the name of Our Lord and Savior, Jesus Christ. Amen.

## The Healing Prayer Ministry

The revelation that God had given me a gift to heal others surprised me. I felt honored and also that I had, to some degree, discovered my truth that this was where I belonged. Perhaps, I thought, maybe I always had this gift and it had been lying latent all my life waiting to reveal itself in God's own time.

I made a conscious commitment to try to understand this mysterious healing power. In the attempt to do so I came to realize that no one can ever truly interpret the mystery of divine love. However, in my zeal, I did try.

Agnes Sanford (1897-1982) the wife of an Episcopal minister) was a pioneer in restoring the charismatic gift of healing to the mainline churches. She became an important influence as I read and devoured everything she wrote. Her understanding of depression came from personal experience.

She had been cured by the healing light of Christ and she believed that Jesus would heal the depression of those wanting it. Her sensitivity and compassion impressed me tremendously, and I hungered to know Scripture as she did. I began to read all the accounts in the four Gospels where Jesus had healed the sick. It seemed he was able to heal people as easily as his preaching of the good news of God's Kingdom on earth. The more I read, the more I was uplifted, and I came to believe that the mission of Jesus was to help us out of our suffering, to make us aware of the Kingdom of God here on earth and the indwelling Spirit within us.

The knowledge that I had this gift puzzled me. To be in a healing ministry was the farthest thought from my mind. Although on one hand I was honored, I also didn't feel worthy of it. There were still had so many issues I was working through, plus, I had a husband and children. Although my marriage was anything but ideal, I still felt a responsibility to keeping it intact. In spite of my sincere efforts the marriage was eventually dissolved.

Father Peter McCall and I met in November 1977. It was a casual meeting on a bus going to a Ruth Carter Stapleton healing service at the Town Hall in New York City. Shortly after this first meeting, Father Peter began to attend the same prayer meeting at the private home where I first discovered I had the gift of healing. Little did we know at the time that we would be swept up into an incredible, adventurous spiritual journey and that it would radically change our lives.

Shortly after we met, I received a phone call from the person at whose home the prayer group met. She asked me to pray for the healing of a teenage boy who had telephoned her. He had heard that there were people in the area who prayed for healing.

She suggested I call Father Peter and invite him to join me since he was interested in learning more about healing prayer, and the caller lived in the vicinity of his parish. Father Peter resided in a Franciscan, Capuchin monastery in Yonkers, was teaching religion and was the athletic director at the Catholic high school associated with the monastery. I made the phone call to Father Peter and we arranged to meet at the young man's home to pray with him. I was very much aware that I didn't know much more than Father Peter did about healing prayer, but I was willing to explore and learn.

We were met at the door by his mother and found he was one of twelve children in a close-knit Polish-American family. The mother appeared so relieved, and appreciative, especially when she saw the priest standing there in his brown robe. She ushered us into the room where her son lay paralyzed from the waist down.

He had been in a devastating car accident. His girlfriend had died in the crash, and the driver of the car had not been hurt seriously. He was angry and depressed and wanted to end his life but changed his mind after watching Christian television. We did pray with him that day and his mother called later to say his spirit seemed to be up-lifted and that he was feeling much better.

We agreed to continue to meet and pray with him. After Father Peter completed his teaching duties at the high school we would meet and pray with this young man one day a week. In time his desire to end his life receded, and he even started to get movement back in his toes.

Unfortunately we could not continue to pray with him when Father Peter had to go out of town for the summer. I had to attend to family commitments, and the boy's family eventually moved from the area. This was the first person Father Peter and I joined together in prayer for a healing.

Soon after, the assistant pastor in my church parish mentioned a young girl about eighteen, (whom I happened to know) who had just been diagnosed with Hodgkin's disease. He asked me if I would be willing to go to the hospital and pray with her. I gladly agreed and asked Father Peter to join us.

We all met at the hospital on a Sunday afternoon with the girl's mother, father, and grandmother. None of them had experienced healing prayer before and did not know what to expect any more than we did. As Father Peter and I explained what we would do, we invited them to join us in prayer.

We began to invoke the name of Jesus and pray for

God's healing power. The girl's mother experienced a jolt of light (energy) entering her own being, and at the same time her daughter felt warmth in her body and a comforting presence. We left them that day with high hopes and expectations of healing and agreed to meet when she returned home to continue healing prayer.

So began the team of Lacy and McCall. Father Peter referred to us as "good old-fashioned doctors" because we made house visits.

We continued to pray with this girl after she was released from the hospital and she began to receive radiation treatments as an out-patient. Following her first treatment, she felt nauseated and could not keep food down. The first time we prayed with her after her treatment we were told by her parents that soon after we left the house, she went to the refrigerator, took out a bowl of spaghetti, heated it up and ate the whole thing. She never had a problem with her appetite or nausea again. Praise God from whom all blessings flow!

During the time she was receiving her radiation treatments we continued the prayer time with her. The X-rays showed improvement time after time. The tumor was shrinking. At one point Father Peter and I were unable to pray with her for about a month due to other commitments. During this time, the technicians who were giving her radiation decided that she was doing so well that they increased the dose of radiation to speed up the healing.

They had assumed that the treatments alone were causing the shrinking of the tumor. They knew nothing about her receiving healing prayer as well. When we returned to continue the prayers with her, we were appalled.

The radiation had burnt her vocal cords and she could not speak. The skin on her chest and back were also badly burned. She was in so much pain, and it hurt us as well to see her like this.

The X-rays showed no visible improvement from the month before. Only during the weeks that she received healing prayer there had been a noticeable improvement. We persevered in praying with her each week and eventually the enlargement disappeared completely. She decided to discontinue the radiation treatments and rely on healing prayer. She eventually went on to live a normal and healthy life.

During the time she was being prayed for, her father, a rugged New York City policeman also experienced a transformation. When we first met him he was rather aloof and austere. As his daughter recovered, he began to soften—I believe he had a spiritual awakening and became more aware of God's love. He joined a Rosary Society in the parish and began to recite the rosary every day and to visit and bring comfort to the sick in the Parish. His daughter was not the only one who was healed.

> Let us pray:
> Loving Lord God, my heart is overflowing with gratitude for you are the Mighty and Holy One who answers our prayers and brings about new life. Out of my distress I called to you. You heard me and helped me. God is my help and my comfort in time of need. Thank you for strengthening me. I praise you for blessing my life with goodness and kindness. Thank you for healing my mind, my heart, my spirit and all that I am or hope to be. Thank you for enriching my life. You have awakened within me a new song of joy and happiness. I will bless and praise your name forever and ever. Amen.

### Bursting Forth

As time went on, we began to receive more and more calls to pray with the sick. It soon became evident that Father Peter could not meet the demands of teaching full time and continue this ministry of healing prayer. In August 1981 he asked permission to resign from teaching and be assigned full time to the healing prayer ministry.

We opened up a Prayer Center and named it The House of Peace. For the next twenty years we witnessed many amazing miracles, as well as some disheartening experiences. I suppose in those twenty years we prayed with thousands of people, and in the process we also had to learn many painful lessons of love and forgiveness.

We developed a program and a newsletter. We held healing Masses, services, workshops and retreats all over the country. We led pilgrimages to Canada, Europe, Mexico, the Caribbean and the Holy Land as well as throughout the United States, and coauthored three books on our experiences with healing prayer.

We called ourselves the Peace of Christ Prayer Ministry, in the belief that the peace of Christ is not only the goal of healing, but also the means. It is in an atmosphere of peace and stillness we can listen within to the voice of the Authentic Healer, the Holy Spirit.

## The Holy Spirit

*"A clean heart create for me, O God and a steadfast spirit renew within me. Cast me not from your presence, and your Holy Spirit take not from me. Give me back the joy of your salvation and a willing spirit sustain in me." (Psalm 51:12-14).*

God has placed within us, at the very core of our being, the answer to every problem. The answer is not a theory or a technique, but a Person, a real Person with a real voice. The Holy Spirit dwells in our minds because it is there that we can choose between sickness and health.

Jesus promised us this Advocate who would speak to us for God and speak to God for us (Jn. 14:26). The Holy Spirit is our "link" to God. The Holy Spirit is the one who is always presenting healing options. By listening to the still gentle voice we will experience healing. We need the power of the Holy Spirit to transform our lives.

## Prayers to the Holy Spirit
(Traditional prayers)

Come Holy Spirit Fill the hearts of your faithful. Enkindle in us the fire of your love. Send forth Your Spirit and we shall be created and You shall renew the face of the earth. Amen.

Holy Spirit:
Replace the tension within us with Holy relaxation.
Replace the turbulence within us with a quiet confidence.
Replace the fear within us with a strong faith.
Replace the bitterness within us with the sweetness of grace.
Replace the coldness within us with loving warmth.
Replace the night within us with your day.
Replace the winter within us with your spring.
Straighten our crookedness, fill our emptiness.
Dull the edge of our pride, sharpen the edge of our humility.
Light the fires of our love. Quench the, flames of our lust
Let us see ourselves as you see us that we may see as you have promised. And be fortunate according to your word.
Blessed are the pure of heart for they shall see God. Amen.

Almighty and eternal God, you have regenerated us by water and the Holy Spirit, and have given us forgiveness for all our sins; send forth from Heaven upon us your sevenfold Spirit: the Spirit of Wisdom and Understanding, the Spirit of Counsel and Fortitude, the Spirit of Knowledge and Piety, the Spirit of Fear (awe) of the Lord. Amen.

## Act of Consecration to The Holy Spirit
(Traditional Catholic prayer)

"Divine Spirit of light and love, I consecrate my mind and heart and will to you for all time and eternity. May my mind be open to your divine inspirations and to the teachings of the Church, whose infallible guide you are. May my heart be filled with love of God and of my neighbor and my will conformed to the will of God. May my whole life be a faithful imitation of the life and virtues of Christ our Lord to who, with the Father and you, be honor and glory forever. Amen."

## What is Healing?
The healing ministry in the mainline churches has been rediscovered in the last century. We say rediscovered because this ministry is as old as Jesus' commission to his disciples, *"Heal the sick." (Mt. 10:7)* Jesus repeats this command after his Resurrection. *"Go into the whole world and proclaim the good news to all creation... Signs like these will accompany those who believe...the sick upon whom they lay their hands will recover." (Mk. 16:15-19)*

The Apostolic Church presumed healing as a normal part of its ministry. The Acts of the Apostles and the Letter of James show that healing was an accepted fact because of the Risen Presence of Jesus in the community.

This expectation that healing through prayer was normal Christian practice began to erode around the fourth century. There were many different and sorry reasons for this decline. One big reason was a theology that arose which said that the miracles and healings of Jesus and the early Christians were only necessary to get the Church started. Once the Church was established, the need for miracles was no longer there. Miracles were simply used as "proof texts" to show that Jesus and the Church were divine. Miracles were seen as "divine gimmicks" to get the attention to prove the validity of the Church.

What happened was that miracles and healings became the domain of the saints to prove their holiness. Canonization of a saint today still demands miracles. Healings were reserved to special people and holy places. The whole idea that healing was God's normal will and an expression of divine compassion was not even considered.

There has been no time in history when people did not seek relief from suffering through prayer. What makes our time different is that the expectancy that prayer can heal has returned. Thanks to the Pentecostal and Charismatic renewals of the churches, "the gift of healing" has been restored as an ordinary *"gift of the Holy Spirit."(1 Cor. 12:9)*

Ordinary people are manifesting this "gift" through the "laying on of hands." The old stereotypical thinking that God wants us to suffer is being challenged. There is a new open-mindedness that accepts the possibility of healing through prayer.

Prayer needs to become a routine part of an overall program for healing. We do not oppose ordinary medical care. All we know is that "prayer works" and ought to be included as a natural part of the healing process. Prayer is not performing magic, but combined with faith and ordinary health care, miracles can and do happen. Praise God!

Father Peter and I had a great deal to learn about healing prayer. In the beginning we thought we were to pray for physical healing only.

The word "healing" can be deceptive. It can be used to describe a situation where a person experiences a temporary relief or removal of obvious symptoms. Many people claim a healing when physical or emotional symptoms disappear. While such a relief from pain or oppression may be welcomed, the removal of symptoms alone does not necessarily show that a healing has taken place.

We know from experience that what seems to be a healing can amount to the transfer of symptoms from one form to another. For example, a person may claim a healing from cigarette smoking only to develop the symptoms of overeating. In this case, the deeper healing failed to occur because the root cause of the addiction was not touched. The symptoms may have changed, but the cause is still present.

*"Be compassionate, as your Father is compassionate. Do not judge and you will not be judged. Do not condemn, and you will not be condemned. Pardon and you shall be pardoned. Give and it will be given you. Good measure, pressed down, shaken together, running over, will they pour into the fold of your garment. For the measure you measure will be measured back to you." (Luke 6:36-37)*

*"Coming down from the mountain with them, he stopped at a level stretch where there were many of his disciples. A large crowd of people was with them from all Judea and Jerusalem and the coast of Tyre and Sidon, people who came to hear him and be healed of their diseases. Those who were troubled with unclean spirits were cured; indeed, the whole crowd was trying to touch him because power came out from him which cured all." (Luke 6:17-20)*

*"His reputation spread more and more, and great crowds gathered to hear him and be cured of their maladies. He often retired to deserted places and prayed." (Luke 5:15-16)*

*"One day Jesus was teaching, and the power of the Lord made him heal." (Luke 5:17)*

Let us pray:
Loving Lord God help us to understand the power of your healing love for us in Christ Jesus. Help us to believe that

Jesus still heals in this day and age under the guidance and influence of the Holy Spirit. You have not abandoned us but have given us a power far greater than any of us can ever imagine. Heal us of the root causes of our infirmities, our guilt and anxieties, our fears, and our stubborn unforgiveness. Grant us faith to believe that you are the One who is able to heal all our ills. In the Holy and Glorious name of Jesus, we pray. Amen.

## The False-Self and the True-Self

The false-self is that part of our personality that sabotages our best interests. It is our defense mechanism to survive in this world. Jesus describes this process when he said that we must deny ourselves and follow him. (Re: Mt. 16:24)

The true meaning of self-denial is dying to our false-self. At the House of Peace we had a slogan: "Healing is not what we do, but what we undo." Just as there is no secret formula to pray for healing, so there is no magical disposition that will guarantee healing.

We should be aware of the obstacles we can set up to resist healing prayer. These obstacles include a sense of unworthiness, a resistance to change, all forms of unforgiveness and bitterness, an unwillingness to participate in the healing process, a death wish, and a sense of resignation to our sickness which sees no alternative way to healing. These obstacles are unconscious in most people, but it is important to look at them with all honesty.

The removal of obstacles is called by the spiritual masters "the way of negation", a way of negating or dying to the false-self. The false-self is the self-image we developed to cope with the emotional trauma of childhood. It seeks happiness in satisfying the instinctual need of survival/security, affection/esteem, and power/control, and bases its self-worth on cultural and group identification.

One of the best ways of undoing the false-self is to enter into the practice of Centering Prayer. Once I know I am embraced and loved by Love itself, I need never be concerned about being other than the person God created me to be.

Our true-self is that image of God in which every human being is created. We learn there is freedom of choice, inner peace, joy and love as we submit to allowing Divine Love to help us and heal us. Our unhappiness is usually caused by the false-self. It is in our best interests to work at the undoing of our false-self if we want to be healed.

Through the many years we ministered healing prayer, we also realized we were being healed. I was being healed of depression, proneness to accidents, stomach ailments, migraine headaches, as well as many fears and anxieties, guilt, and shame.

These healings manifested gradually over a period of time. I would one day notice that a particular ailment had disappeared. Thank you, Lord God! As we taught healing prayer, we also were learning.

One of the major lessons we had to learn was that the very root of all healing is forgiveness. Forgiveness on every level is essential to the healing process. We must forgive God, ourselves, and others if we expect to become whole and well. God wants us to be free in body, mind, soul and spirit, more than we want it ourselves. We are invited to be healed of our anger, fears, guilt, shame, and hurts.

As we allow the love of Christ to heal our wounds, we open ourselves to a wonderful new way of living life and of relating to ourselves and others. God is perfect love, there is no other!

## Prayer for the Healing of Guilt and Shame

Blessed be the Lord in whom I place my trust. O wondrous and magnificent Lord God I come before you with a willing heart. I so desire to become who YOU want me to be. I want to die to that false part of me and become ever present to my true reality. Help me now as I agree with you to enter into a commitment to myself and accept your help in the dying and rising to new life. I pray the Holy Spirit will guide me in the path of Truth.

O Lord, there have been so many times in my life when feelings of shame would overwhelm me. This shame has been a destructive force in my life and keeps me in bondage to the past. I long to be set free from the negative memories of that which shaped how badly I feel about myself. I come before you now asking to be set free by the power of your love. Only you, O loving Lord God can heal the pain I am in. My heart has been broken so many times throughout my life. There have been so many separations, times when I felt abandoned.

Sometimes I have felt as though no one could ever love me. I humbly place myself before you, acknowledging fully that I am in great need of your love. I need your healing power to bring me inner peace. You are the only one who can bless my life with the consolations and peace of mind I need.

Help me to see myself the way you see me. Help me now to believe in myself and in your sweet, sweet love for me. Show me how to undo the negatives I feel about myself. I so desire to know and accept your loving will in my life. Show me how to forgive, O Lord. Show me how to be still and know that you love me with an everlasting love that will never leave me.

Show me how to forgive myself and help me to release all

these feelings of shame and dread help me to let go of self-hatred and self-destructive tendencies. Help me to drop my false self-image and repent from self-deception. Show me how to forgive those people in my life who have made me feel less than a beautiful child of God.

I let go of anyone living or deceased who has been the cause of shaming me and has hurt me the most. Lord, I want to let go of the burden of guilt

I carry in my soul a longing...I yearn to be set free. You 0 Lord are my only hope, my true salvation. In your great kindness rescue me and help me to see the truth about myself. I thank you for the awareness that I am under your loving guidance and protection. As a precious gift to this world, I am assured by your love that I can never be put to shame again, for I place my trust in you.

In Scripture we learn that Jesus wants us to be free of all burdens. His words are so sweet... "Come to me, all you who weary and find life burdensome, and I will refresh you. Take my yoke upon your shoulders and learn from me, for I am gentle and humble of heart. Your souls will find rest, for my yoke is easy and my burden light."

Thank you Lord Jesus, so gentle and kind and thank you for lifting the burden of guilt and shame from my mind so that I, too, may find rest. I acknowledge and affirm that the Lord holds me in high esteem. I believe I will be healed. I shall be completely restored in body, mind and spirit by the wonderful grace of Almighty God. May the Glory of the Lord endure forever. Amen.

O Lord, my God, I come before you now to ask your pardon. I have been led to believe you are a God to be feared. I have not seen you through the eyes of wonder and awe but rather as a God who is judgmental and critical. I believed I had to beg and plead in order to be heard by you. I believed that I was so imperfect, so flawed that you could not possibly love me. I believed that if I made mistakes and was not perfect, I would be punished by you.

My fears have crippled and terrorized me. I cry out to you in my mistaken thinking, 0 Loving Savior help me and heal me. Memories of oppression plague me. I grew up feeling you were a hard taskmaster and so was deathly afraid of you. My false-self kept me believing you were like those people who were in authority over me and who taught me you were a God who scrutinized every mistake and caused pain through retaliation.

Loving Lord God, show me how to let you draw me to yourself with love and acceptance and to let you dissolve my fears. Help me to remember that I have nothing to fear from you who love me perfectly.

0 God I believe you have already granted me the pardon I seek as I am being made aware of your unconditional love. Scripture tells me that your perfect love will cast my fears far from me. I pray to be set free daily from any former tendencies, believing in lies rather than your sweet love for me.

My frightened inner child surfaces many times and finds it difficult to embrace the notion of a God who loves tenderly and wholly. Heal the child within and set me free from spiritual impoverishment. Set me free from the temptations of sin and self-destructive thoughts. In the past self hatred led me to try to ease the fears and anxieties I felt.

I would turn to all types of wrong behaviors, such as: (fill in here with your own habits or proneness to addictions-for example...(overeating, alcohol, wrong relationships, gambling, drugs or raging). O Lord, I was not in my right mind and am ashamed of the ways in which I tried to numb my pain. 0 Lord you know me through and through. You know O Lord and understand and are cheering me on, rooting for me. I choose to believe that you are intimately concerned for my highest good.

You are perfect love, there is no other! You are an Infinite Wellspring of loving kindness. You are the Great Giver of all goodness and mercy. I truly repent of my wrong thinking and actions. Help me to forgive myself: Free me from the regrets of the past. Help me to know that in this present moment you are gazing on me with love and compassion.

I am willing to consent to be made aware of your constant love for me. Show me how to be still and know that I am worthy of your loving me. Help me to dissolve the walls of fear as I consent to being loved by you more and more. I acknowledge and affirm that I am slowly learning how to love myself in healthy ways with the help of the Holy Spirit.

I am beginning to experience what it really means to be a precious child of the most high and awesome God. I come before you in gratitude and peace with a new awareness of your absolute goodness. I thank you with all my heart and soul. Blessed be your name forever and ever. Amen.

# Chapter 3

## Healing our Self-Esteem

### We are each a special creation of GOD

*"The soul of man, left to its own natural level, is a potentially lucid crystal left in darkness. It is perfect in its own nature, but it lacks something that it can only receive from outside and above itself. But when the light shines in it, it becomes in a manner transformed into light and seems to lose its nature in the splendor of a higher nature, the nature of the light that is in it.*

*"So that natural goodness of man, his capacity for love which must always be in some sense selfish if it remains in the natural order, becomes transfigured and transformed when the Love of God shines in it." -Thomas Merton*

Participating in a lifelong process of undoing the causes and effects of low self-worth requires work in the healing of self-esteem. Having been in a healing prayer ministry for well over three decades, I came up with a theory of my own. I came to believe that Jesus, our Redeemer, wants to make it up to us for every time we were wounded physically, spiritually and emotionally. It has been my experience that he wants to love us back to life.

We have to come to a decision and take the risk of faith and courage, and at some point, prepare to open ourselves to the healing process.

Throughout the years I was in ministry I heard too many stories of childhood abuses where thoughtless and insensitive comments made by adults squelched the creativity and spontaneity of children. Almost everyone has had some experience of being maltreated.

A woman came to our prayer center for healing and shared that she had been thoughtlessly shamed in front of the class when in the second grade she had raised her hand to go to the bathroom and the teacher refused to let her go. She recalled the terrible embarrassment when she wet herself and the resulting incriminations. The shame of it plagued her and now being able to voice how she felt as we prayed with her, helped defuse the negative power she felt within. The love she experienced through the prayer healed the memory of that time.

Unfortunately I have heard even worse stories of emotional, physical, verbal, and sexual abuse. These range in various degrees and are debilitating to a young person's psyche often with life-long consequences. Fortunately there is hope with the help of programs that include counseling, healing prayer, forgiveness, twelve step spirituality and other forms of healing modalities and treatments.

We all are aware of celebrities who are adored by their fans and have talents, good looks, are popular and have many material possessions yet cannot get through life without alcohol or drugs. Too many do not have a solid footing from their early childhood years.

Many give their power away to others because they believe they do not have a voice or opinion of their own that is worth much. They look for approval from people they admire rather than realizing their own true self-worth.

It has been our experience in the healing prayer ministry that the many people who came to us for healing were stricken with a devastating self-hatred. Most people who abuse or hurt themselves with drugs, alcohol, eating disorders and other substances have not the slightest idea that they are SPIRITUAL BEINGS AND THE PRESENCE of God is within them. They have no clue that in self-destructing they are lessening their spiritual dimension, the essence of who they are. Too many of God's beloved people are holding themselves back from the fullness and joy of life because of low self-esteem.

*"Love justice, you who judge the earth; think of the Lord in goodness, and seek him in integrity of heart; because he is found by those who test him not, and he manifests himself to those who do not disbelieve him." (The book of Wisdom 1:1-2)*

We used to pray with a man who had multiple sclerosis. Father Peter suggested that he see a psychologist friend of his since this gentleman didn't seem to be making any progress spiritually or physically. Yet I felt he must have received something because he kept coming back week after week.

The psychologist eventually gave a report to Father Peter and said that he had never come across someone who was so lacking in self-esteem that he didn't even have a sense of self. This particular gentleman was knockout handsome and had been a lawyer prior to his illness but had always felt less than who he truly was.

No one had ever told him that he was a treasure and a precious child of God. I do feel though that he liked the attention and love we gave him through our prayers even though he was not healed physically. It is impossible to count the losses of goodness and light to the world. The reason being: too many people feel they are unlovable and have nothing to offer.

Let us pray:

Blessed Savior, Holy One, we need and depend on your sweet love to make up to us all the pain and disrespect we were subjected to as little children. We have felt badly about ourselves. The memories remain and sometimes we can hardly hold our head up for the shame we have experienced.

At times life seems just too harsh and depression overtakes us. Dear Lord, we ask you to heal the little child within us. We need reminders of your care and concern for us. We need to hear how special and precious we are in your sight. Send us spiritual Mothers and Fathers, brothers and sisters who will encourage and affirm us. We need you, O loving Lord, to remind us of who we really are.

Free us from feelings of worthlessness and shame and self-doubt. By the power of your unconditional love, heal our minds and our spirits. Your love and grace are all we need. Heal our memories and soften the impact of the violence done to our fragile minds and souls. Touch us with your powerful love so that we may feel and experience your sweetness, your gentleness, your warm, approving gaze.

We need to know you, and love you, for Scripture tells us you know us and love us infinitely. We yearn for your life to fill us. We need your love to melt away the fears and anxieties that make us unhealthy, weak and depressed. Help us to believe in ourselves, and our true worth, for you have deemed us worthy, through your sacrificial love for us. Thank you for hearing our plea for help, 0 most loving Lord, Jesus. Blessed be your holy name forever and ever. Amen.

Scripture tells us of how Jesus affirms us and makes astounding claims about us, *"You are the salt of the*

*earth! What if salt goes flat? How can you restore its fla-*
*vor, then it is good for nothing." He goes on to say, "You*
*are the Light of the world! A City set on a hill cannot be*
*hidden. Men do not light a lamp and set it under a bushel*
*basket. They set it on a stand where it can give light to*
*all in the house. In the same way your Light must shine*
*before all so that they may see goodness in your acts and*
*give glory to God." (Mt. 5:1)*

Building healthy self-esteem takes time and patience
with oneself. There are really no set rules as to how to go
about it, although once we make the decision to become
healthy, the Holy Spirit will be there with the guidance
we need. Becoming aware of how precious we are comes
about by allowing ourselves to consider and experience
God's unconditional love.

How that may happen depends on each person's willingness to be open to the experience. Old fears and habits are blocks to the awareness of that love. If we do not
see ourselves as loveable or we are stuck in self-depreca-
tion, this is another obstacle that needs healing so that
we may be brought into that glorious light of Jesus. He
beckons us to draw close to Him.

Bill Wilson, the cofounder of Alcoholics Anonymous,
was considered a lost cause. His alcoholism was so severe it was killing him, mentally and physically. In the
"Life of Bill Wilson" in the Big Book, Part 10 of 12: The
Spiritual Journey 1895-1934, we read: Wilson rode high
throughout the roaring twenties fueled by the soaring
stock market and by bootleg gin. The market crashed
in 1929 and Bill's final collapse came five years later.
By then he was diagnosed a chronic alcoholic laying in
detox for the fourth time within a year.

He writes: "My depression deepened unbearably and
finally it seemed to me as though I were at the very bottom of the pit. I still gagged very badly on the notion
of a Power greater than myself, but finally, just for the

moment, the last vestige of my proud obstinacy was crushed. All at once I found myself crying out, `If there is a God, let Him show Himself! I am ready to do anything, anything!'

"Suddenly the room lit up with a great white light. I was caught up in an ecstasy which there are no words to describe. It seemed to me, in the mind's eye, that I was on a mountain and that a wind not of air but of spirit was blowing. And then it burst upon me that I was a free man. Slowly the ecstasy subsided.

"I lay on the bed, but now for a time I was in another world, a new world of consciousness. All about me and through me there was a wonderful feeling of Presence.

And I thought to myself, `So this is the God of the preachers!' A great peace stole over me and I thought, `No matter how wrong things may seem to me, they are still all right. Things are all right with God and His world."

This spiritual encounter shook Wilson to the core of his soul and changed him forever. Spiritually, he returned to the experience over and over again throughout his life drawing strength and solace from it when nothing else seemed able to satisfy him.

He rarely gave an AA talk without revisiting his "white light" experience and sharing the story over and over again with countless alcoholics who desperately needed and waited for their own souls to be touched and healed by whatever light Wilson had found in that hospital room.

Bill would spend the rest of his life carrying that message of experience, strength and hope and building a worldwide fellowship based on his spiritual experience.

Jesus has proclaimed, *"I am the Light of the world. No follower of mine shall ever walk in darkness; no, he shall possess the light of life." (Jn. 8:12)*

Let us pray:
Blessed be the name of our Lord and Savior, Jesus Christ, now and forever. Blessed be the holy one of Israel. Blessed be Jesus Christ, Son of the Living God, the Light of the world. Blessed be his wondrous deeds. Blessed be the Prince of Peace. Blessed be the beloved Savior of our lives. Blessed be the One who has sanctified us. Blessed be the maker of miracles. Blessed be Jesus Christ, true God and true man. Blessed be his wondrous Love. Blessed be His Holy Presence. Glory be to the Father and to the Son and to the Holy Spirit, now and forever. Amen.

It was a long time after Father Peter died that I felt strong enough emotionally to continue this work of healing. So stunned was I by his sudden death, it literally took my breath away. Feeling the loss deep in my soul I was traumatized, disheartened and lifeless, believing I had nothing left to give.

I had identified myself for so many years with being in a healing ministry and working for God that I had forgotten who I really was. Leaving all that I knew and taking an indefinite sabbatical was the only consideration I felt I had at the time.

For a long while I remained in a limbo state... I didn't seem to belong anywhere. Too much grief and loss had permeated my life. It was all I could do to get through each day trusting God to help me. I had depended on Father Peter's priesthood and his authority in the church to legitimize my spiritual gifts.

I did not feel secure enough as a Catholic lay woman, to do the work of healing in the church without the authority of the priesthood. It didn't dawn on me right away, nor did it phase me when it did, to realize that God had validated me long before I had met Father Peter.

My inner child remembered only the negative... I had

been given a different set of instructions that led me to believe that I was not good enough. That hurt, under-valued, frightened little girl was still there; sitting in the semi-darkness of my unconscious all these many years, reluctant, yet wanting by the grace of the Holy Spirit, to be set free, to discover another level of her truest self. The false-self had come out of hiding to reveal its nasty nature. Thankfully I had been given and, gratefully re-ceived, the tools of faith, and trust in a loving God in order to bring about the healing I needed.

One of my favorite saints, St. Catherine of Siena, the great mystic and doctor of the Church in the fourteenth century, had many conversations with God. She wrote them in a book called, *The Dialogue.* God instructs Cath-erine that we are to dwell in the "cell of self-knowledge."

God speaks to Catherine and to us saying, "Be care-ful never to leave the cell of self-knowledge, but in this cell guard and spread the treasure I give you. This trea-sure is a teaching of truth founded in the living rock, the gentle Christ Jesus clothed in a light than can dis-cern darkness. Clothe yourself in this light, dearest one whom I so love in truth."

Our souls yearn to seek the truth and our minds thirst for knowledge of who we really are. Jesus speaks to the woman at the well concerning the well-springs of living water that can rise within us to give us new life.

*"Whoever drinks the water I give will never be thirsty; no, the water I give shall become a fountain within, leap-ing up to provide eternal life." (Jn. 4:14).*

Let us pray:
Praise God from whom all blessings flow! Praise him all creatures here below. Praise him above you heavenly hosts. Praise the God of unconditional love. Thank you Blessed Savior now and forever. We praise your holy name. You are freeing us from self-doubt and saving us from deception.

You are the life-giving water that restores our minds and our spirits. May your living water satisfy the thirst in our souls, ever yearning for the knowledge of your love for us. Help us now to enter into that cell of self-knowledge so we may discover the beauty and truth within ourselves as we are learning to understand that you are a God of unending beauty and truth. Blessed be the name of the Lord now and forever. Amen.

## The False-Self

Spiritual healing comes about by entering into the process of "the cell of self-knowledge." In doing so we will come to recognize the characteristics of what Thomas Merton coined, "the False-Self."

The false-self is called by many names and takes many forms. However, its basic characteristic is a negative self-image which we have accepted as true and which has power over us because we continue to believe in it. This negative belief is unconscious, but is reinforced by decisions made in accord with its viewpoint.

The false-self is the sum total of all the negative decisions we have made about ourselves based on past associations. It is the self we learned and created in order to survive this world.

Theologians would call the false-self the result of "original sin." Psychologists would describe it as "deprivation neurosis." Probably the best description of it comes from Carl Jung when he referred to it as our "shadow."

No matter what you call it, it is a very powerful belief and should never be underestimated. It is as powerful as the faith we put into it, a premise from which we draw many conclusions. The false-self is made up of what I have, what I do and what people think of me.

The false-self believes that it is separated from God and will be punished for this separation. This is usually accompanied by feelings of guilt and anxiety. It believes it is deprived of what it needs and that it suffers loss every time it gives something away.

Love is for those who do what it wants, and hate is for those who do not do what it wants. It also believes God loves some people more than others and that it must earn God's love.

Competition is the way to prove the worth and value of a person. Control and manipulation are the ways to get things done, and that means a future just like the past. Change in its own mind is resisted. The outside world must change for it to be happy.

Punishment is appropriate reparation for sin and sacrifice is the way to appease an angry God. Salvation is concerned only with the physical. It believes only in this world and that success or failure is to be judged by the world's standards.

Because the false-self believes that something is inherently wrong, guilt forms its bedrock. Since guilt is painful, it will try to relieve this pain. It uses two techniques or defense mechanisms to do this.

This first is to simply deny that any guilt exists. This is what is known in psychology as repression. It plays the ostrich and hides its head in the sand at the sight of danger and then believes it is safe. This does not always work, so it relies on a second technique.

The second technique is projection. This technique simply dumps the responsibility for its guilt onto some scapegoat. This is the foundation and justification for anger. It finds someone to whom it can self-righteously say, "If only you were different, I would be happy." This is why the false-self needs to maintain love/hate relationships. Because the false-self is based on a low self-image, it is defensive and a faultfinder. It thrives on competition and comparisons. It needs to find people worse off to make itself feel good.

It has a "holier than thou" attitude and is ready to cast into hell anyone who disagrees with it. It is a master of deception and a father of lies.

I had been asked to speak to a Cancer Support group at a local hospital. The people in the group were in various stages of cancer and treatment.

I gave a teaching on healing prayer and shared some meaningful experiences. Then I offered to pray with anyone in the group who would like to have the experience. One or two declined because of religious beliefs and left. I went around to the remaining group of people one on one and asked what they would like me to pray for.

As I prayed with each person it surprised me that no one asked for a healing or a cure of cancer for themselves. Each person prayed for ordinary things such as a family problem or for a relative or friend that was in some sort of difficulty.

Only one woman prayed that she would not lose her teeth as a result of chemotherapy. I left that evening and was saddened even though I knew I had done my best to help. I had to trust that whatever healing was needed that night, it was sufficient for each person according to their faith.

*"Your faith has restored you." (Mt. 10:22)*

Let us pray:
0 Loving Lord God, the false self holds us back from believing the truth, the truth that will set us free. We need your saving power, 0 loving Lord. We want for desire of your healing touch. You are the only one we can turn to for the help we need. We are lost without you. We are kept in captivity by the false self. It does not want us to know the truth about your love for us. The false self wants us to remain blind to the light and goodness that is within.

The false self deceives us in order to keep us bound to its

lies. We need your truth, your life, your love and we need your blessing. Teach us how to forgive ourselves for the imperfections we see within.

We need to forgive ourselves for failing to be the person who you have called us to be. Teach us to forgive others for their humanness and help us to forgive those who have hurt us even when we feel they don't deserve it.

Your grace is sufficient, your goodness much greater than my petty perceptions. Grant us the grace to choose your will for us for you are our Creator and you know what will be most helpful in order to bring us the inner peace we seek. Restore us and bring us into the fullness of life Thank you for being patient with us, and help us to be patient with ourselves as we continue the journey back to our higher selves. We love you Lord, Jesus and we place our trust in you. Blessed be your name now and forever. Amen.

## Co-Dependency

Co-dependency is part and parcel of the false-self system. It is a pattern of learned behaviors that makes life painful. It is the reaction to dysfunctional family systems that exaggerate our need to control, our need for external validation, our dependency issues and self neglect. It is a loss of identity and self-esteem which sets up enmeshments, isolation and/or over responsibility in relationships.

Co-dependency produces confusion, denial, anxiety, depression, shame and excess guilt as well as compulsive, self-destructive behaviors and stress-related illnesses.

These are some of the general characteristics of co-dependency:

- Having an over developed responsibility. It is easier for us to be concerned with others than ourselves. This in turn has enabled us not to look too closely at our faults.
- We stuff our feelings from our traumatic childhoods and lose the ability to feel or express our feelings because it hurts too much.
- We tend to put the wants and needs of others before our own.
- We want approval from others; thus losing our own identity.
- We have to be needed in order to have a relationship with others.
- We assume responsibility for other people's behaviors or feelings.
- We tend to love people we can pity and rescue.
- We avoid and are frightened by angry people.
- We are terrified of abandonment, holding on to painful relationships.
- We tend to see ourselves as martyrs or victims of the world around us.
- We feel guilty if we stand up for ourselves.
- We often don't know how we feel.

Like every illness, co-dependency has degrees. Not every co-dependent personality has to go to therapy or go to meetings. In many cases, good teaching combined with prayer is enough to make the person aware. Being aware is the beginning of the healing.

At the heart of the disease of co-dependency is the learned belief that we get our value and worth as persons from outside ourselves. Co-dependents are addicted to relationships from which they perceive they get their identity. Co-dependents make themselves indispensable because they want to be needed. They will do anything to maintain a relationship, even at the expense of their health and happiness.

Because co-dependency is an identity issue, healing prayer can provide an appropriate place where we can get in touch with fundamental beliefs and assumptions which we have accepted about ourselves. It is a learned response to the world around us. The fact that it is learned means it can be unlearned.

So much of healing has nothing to do with what we do but what we undo. Letting go of self- destructive beliefs is where healing begins.

Co-dependency, like all addictions, is a spiritual disease. Through the power of the Holy Spirit we can defuse the destructive power of shame and self-hatred. Through healing prayer, we will discover that we are loved and accepted just because we are precious children of God. God's unconditional love will heal our shame. We do not have to pretend or perform anymore in order to receive love and approval.

We begin to understand who we really are, that we are radically good because our source is All Good. We do not have to hide our inner selves anymore because God knows us and loves us anyway. We can let go of the hurts of the past because the present moment of grace is more powerful than anything that came before it. The only thing that is asked of us is the willingness to accept God's unconditional love.

Let us pray:
Loving Lord God, we need the grace to believe in ourselves and be freed from the self-doubt and insecurities that plague us. We need to be healed from the root cause of why we feel badly about ourselves. We ask and pray for your overflowing love to filter through the inner core of our souls and touch

those areas of our lives that were so deeply wounded and we believed we were less than nothing. Heal us and love us back to life so that we may no longer feel our worth is in being used by others. Set us free from the need to be needed. This deception is sabotaging our emotional and physical health. We are so weary and would like to develop healthy relationships. Set us free dear Lord from the tendency to set ourselves up with people who would take advantage of our good nature just because we want to feel loved. We need to believe that you desire our happiness. Show us how to become more open and honest with ourselves. Show us how to develop a healthy self-respect and to treat others with respect. Teach us how to give and receive in a healthy way, not at the expense of ourselves and our health. Show us how to balance our lives and to ultimately be true to ourselves. We ask this in the name above all names, Our Lord and Savior, Jesus Christ. Let it be done by the power of the Holy Spirit. Amen and Amen.

## Some of the Signs of Low Self-Esteem

- A negative and hopeless view of yourself, your family and society.
- A preference for being alone, not wanting to meet new people.
- Keeping others away, having trouble making friends.
- Avoiding looking into the eyes of others...shame based.
- Difficulty with genuine trust, intimacy and affection and in extreme cases being anti-social.
- An unwillingness or inability to set or achieve goals,
- Fear of speaking up for yourself. Self-doubt.
- Refusing to take risks, a fear of failure or of success.
- Tending to be negative, speaking negatively

about yourself.
- Tending to be hard on yourself, not forgiving yourself or others.
- Feelings of worthlessness, that other people are better than you
- Envy, because others have more than you.
- Having no compassion or remorse, because you are unaware of your own feelings.
- Not smiling easily and tending to be unhappy about yourself and life in general.
- A low opinion of yourself.
- Feelings of insecurity and lack of self-confidence.
- Having a victim or martyr complex.
- Wanting to be needed in order to receive acceptance and approval
- Tendency to focus on yourself and analyze why you are the way you are.
- Feelings of guilt and not knowing why.
- Neglecting your physical appearance.
- You are tired a great deal of the time...depressed.
- Generally just feeling bad about you.

## The True-Self

The true-self is that part of us that knows that we are as God created us.

*"...in His image and likeness," (Gen. 1:26)* and *"He looked at His creation and said, 'It is very good.'" (Gen. 1:31)*

The true self knows itself as innately good and claims its rightful inheritance as a child of God in the Kingdom of God.

Jesus said, *"Every good tree bears good fruit." (Mt. 7:17)*

Since the true self begins with a belief in goodness, its characteristics will be good. The true self believes that it is always one with God and that separation from the Divine is impossible.

*"What God has joined together, let no one separate."* *(Mt. 19:6)*

The true-self lacks nothing from God, and has already received what it needs even before it asks for it. (Re: Mt. 6:32)

The true self believes all people are equally loved by God and that Love is unconditional.

*"All things are possible to God."* *(Mt. 19:26)* and the Holy Spirit's interpretation of this world is available to everyone. *"Your verdict on others will be the verdict passed on you."* *(Mt. 7:2)* It believes gifts are increased as they are given away and that we receive in proportion to what we share. *"It is mercy I desire and not sacrifice."* *(Mt. 12:7)* God is not pleased with sacrifice, *"I will take delight in doing good to them: I will replant them in this land with all my heart and soul."* *(Jer. 32:41)* God delights in doing only good for his creation.

*"Jesus said, 'Father, forgive them; they do not know what they are doing.'"* *(Lk. 23:34)* All forgiveness is deserved because violent people are insane and do not know what they are doing.

The true-self can accept responsibility for the world around it and trust in the Holy Spirit's guidance. *"Be on your guard with respect to others."* *(Mt. 10:17)* The true-self is not a Pollyanna. It does, however, rely on the interpretation of the Holy Spirit to see all things through *"the mind of Christ."* *(1 Cor. 2:16)*

Both the false-self and the true-self interpret what we see. They are two voices which are trying to get our attention. The authentic voice of the Holy Spirit teaches us the truth. We do not deny what our physical eyes see, rather we allow the Holy Spirit to be the "Advocate," the *"Spirit of Truth,"* *(Jn. 14:17)* who can help us to see things clearly and make wise choices.

Healthy self-esteem is an achievement, a process that

empowers, energizes and motivates. It is becoming your own best self. The National Association for Self-Esteem describes it as the experience of being capable of meeting life's challenges and feeling worthy of happiness.

## Some Definitions of Healthy Self-Esteem

- Seeing yourself in a realistic and loving way.
- Knowing you are not perfect but accepting yourself as you are.
- Feeling comfortable with yourself, your values, likes, dislikes, dreams and choices.
- The awareness that God loves you creates peace within yourself.
- Having a good opinion about yourself, being your own best friend.
- Having a positive attitude. Seeing the good within yourself and others.
- Believing in, and having confidence in your self.
- Having an appreciation and participating fully in the joy of life.
- Being engaged in worthwhile pursuits, doing good for others without expecting repayment.
- Having self-assurance.
- Having a self-caring program.
- Saying no when you mean no and yes when you mean yes
- Having and knowing your boundaries.
- Forgiving yourself when you make a mistake.
- Having an attitude of gratitude.
- Being on time and keeping appointments.
- Capable of making decisions based on intelligent guidance.
- Spending time in prayer and meditation.
- Most of all... being patient with oneself along with the process.

## Self Caring

As part of the healing of our self-esteem we need to incorporate a self-caring program. We must understand
that it is not selfish to take care of oneself. This is a
much misunderstood concept that needs to be corrected.

At a conference we were giving, we were discussing
this topic about being self-caring, when an Irish woman
interrupted us to say that she had been taught differently, that to be self-caring was selfish.

The idea of self-caring does not mean being self-centered. It simply means that we need to take time to see
to it that our physical, mental, spiritual and emotional
needs are met. In order to remain healthy we need to live
a balanced life.

This is especially important if we have to take care
of others. We need to get enough sleep, healthy food and
exercise taking time to walk in a nature, or reading a
good book, or fun times with friends. We need to keep
our minds alert with healthy mental stimulation. We
take time to explore ways in which we can be spiritually
in tune with our Creator.

We may need to talk things over with a spiritual director or a mature spiritual person, someone to guide us
in the spiritual life. Through a self-caring program we
can find the peace within that is absolutely necessary to
maintain equilibrium.

We don't need to compare ourselves with others or be
competitive. We can do things for other people because
we want to, and not to get something in return. We are
learning it is alright to share love with others and allow
others to share their love with us.

Giving is receiving. Self-caring people tend to find
the love and attention they need first and are then able
to give to others. We spend time with people who respect
us so we can have emotional stability. We cannot expect
any one person or  a group to meet all our needs.

In order to be self-caring, we learn to understand our limitations and the limitations of others. We seek the serenity and peace we need and realize our own true self-worth. Yet we allow others the dignity of making their own mistakes and enjoying their achievements.

We develop humility in recognizing that we are neither the greatest in the world nor the least, but that we are precious people in the Kingdom of the most high and magnificent God. We are vital to the plan of salvation by acknowledging our own true self-worth and by taking good care of ourselves.

*"You must know that your body is a temple of the Holy Spirit, who is within, the Spirit you have received from God. You are not your own. You have been purchased, and at a price. So glorify God in your body." (1 Cor. 6:19-20)*

We never stop learning. We are always learning, growing in the process of becoming the beautiful, grand person God created us to be.

Let us pray:
0 Most loving, most high God, we are searching for the truth within our hearts and minds, as we seek your ways, in order to know your will. Sometimes we suffer from anxiety and worry. We are unsure of ourselves and the direction our lives are pointing to. We want to be made aware of the ways in which we are being selfish, and self-centered.

We need to be set free from the need to control, and manipulate our lives, and the lives of others. Only by divine grace can we be made aware of our faults. At times we find ourselves fearful of the future so we become grasping, mean and greedy. 0 Lord of love, grant us the grace to repent of our selfishness. There are times when we are most aware of our wrong actions, and we become ashamed.

We wallow in that shame, and we turn our faces from you, rather than turning towards you for the healing we need. Show us how to embark on the path of self-caring. Teach us how to balance our lives so that we may overcome our unruly emotions.

Show us the way to true humility. Help us to accept ourselves and others with all our faults and strengths, the way you accept us. You love us just as we are. We are embarking on a path that hopefully leads to our becoming our true selves. Grant us the vigilance and patience we need to control our thoughts and emotions and to remain calm in the face of crisis.

Help us to trust you in all things; in all the comings and goings of our daily living. Guide us in a self-caring program so that we may be healthy, spiritually, physically, emotionally and in all our relationships.

Help us to be freed from negativity as we seek out those positive people who will be our companions on the road to health. We thank you and bless you for believing in us, loving us, and guiding us in your ways.

We need but, listen and learn as your constant love reveals to us our true and sacred selves. Blessed be your name forever and ever. Glory to God! Glory! Amen.

## Healing Affirmations

- God loves me because God can only love.
- I am God's beloved child, there is no limit to what the Lord can do for me.
- God is with me now and forever.
- I am in God and God is in me.
- The Kingdom of God dwells within me.
- God is holy. I am holy.

- Today is a new gift from God, I choose to undo the past.
- I face today, confident and unafraid because God has a plan for me.
- All I need is already given me since I have God's spirit within me.
- I bring my mistakes out of darkness and place them in the light of God's truth.
- The solution to all my problems is the love of Jesus.
- God has declared me worthy of love.
- I accept God's love for me.
- Now I am one with God who is my soul's desire.
- Being faithful to prayer I am open to receiving God's love.
- God awaits my willingness to receive and give love.
- I accept the gifts given me and the power to use them.
- I am predisposed to miracles.
- The light of Christ shines in me and in all whom I meet.
- Peace is with me wherever I go because Jesus is with me.
- God's unconditional love for me drives away my fear.
- I am being transformed by the grace of God.
- I walk in gratitude, the way of love.
- I am gentle because I know the Source of my strength.
- I am courteous, grateful and generous.
- I choose victory over adversity.
- I believe in peace. I am peaceful.
- I am humble and grateful because I am infinitely loved.
- The Holy Spirit is with me, helping me now.

- I am one with God. God is one with me.
- Jesus is the Master of my heart and soul.

I have given retreats on this particular theme: Restoring our Self-Esteem. Some of those who attended responded with comments to the above affirmations declaring them to be most helpful in reminding them of the truth.

Jesus tells us, *"You will know the truth and the truth will set you free." (Jn. 8:32)*

Maggie Myhal sent me a note saying, "I get so much from the affirmations especially the affirmation 'There is no limit to what God can do for me.' It broadens my view of God."

Jane Byrne wrote, "God loves me because God can only love", this affirmation is something that I have to remind myself over and over so it gets from my head to my heart...then everything else is put in proper perspective.

"'God has a plan for me.' 'God awaits my willingness to receive and give love.' This helps me to remember to always ask in any situation... What is the most loving thing to do?

"'I believe that the Holy Spirit is with me, helping me now.' This helps me not to be fearful because I am never alone and God wants to guide, help and direct me in all I do and all I have to do is get out of God's way."

Jane Grode wrote, "Dear Maryanne, I am an avid affirmation user. I remember my conversion experience via Phil. 4:13, 'I can do all things through Christ who strengthens me.' That verse was my affirmation for months, through the most difficult time in my life. I have used these and other affirmations repeatedly as a moving mantra to be repeated throughout the day, days or even longer. Instead of a sacred word as in centering prayer, the affirmation becomes a sacred phrase.

"I have even written the one I've been working with on a small piece of paper or card and carry it with me to remind me of the message and the healing. With the nature of the mind to wander, and oftentimes in a negative way, I find that by coming back to the affirmation, I am again able to focus on a special message God has selected for me and it brings me that peace that is beyond all understanding. It doesn't matter if I am in the quiet of my home or in a traffic jam...especially in a traffic jam. It works and has changed my whole day. All God's love."

Let us pray:
Loving Lord God, we thank you for affirming us with your unconditional love. You alone are our true happiness, our joy. We join with your holy mind and leave our fears behind. Peace and joy are our inheritance as your precious children.

We seek only that which is of your kingdom for this is our right and you have deemed it so. We choose to lay aside all fears and conflicts and instead choose your life within us. We let go of the deceptions of the past and take on the truth of who we really are in this now moment.

Thank you for restoring our self esteem and our self worth. Thank you for the peace that only you can supply. We desire a life of contentment and bliss. We come to you in confidence this day clearing our minds of selfish thoughts and choose to think holy thoughts.

We desire to follow your holy will for us and want only the grace that leads to eternity with you now and forever. You are our love and our true happiness and joy. Lead us on, O loving Lord God. Amen.

*"The Lord is the Spirit, and where the Spirit of the Lord is, there is freedom. All of us, gazing on the Lord's*

*glory with unveiled faces, are being transformed from glo-*
*ry to glory into his very image the Lord who is the Spirit."*
*(2 Cor. 3:17-18)*

# Chapter 4

The Truth Will Set You Free

Healing our Image of God

*"Hark! My lover... here he comes springing across the mountains, leaping across the hills. My lover is like a gazelle or a young stag; here he stands behind our wall, gazing through the windows, peering through the lattices, my lover speaks; he says to me, 'Arise my beloved, my beautiful one, and come! For see the winter is past, the rains are over and gone'." (Song of Songs 2:8b-11)*

There is no authentic healing without change at some level in our lives. In order to practice the Presence of God, our image of God may have to be corrected. What needs to be corrected will come out in the healing process as we open ourselves to new ideas and alternatives.

When we have a fearful image of God, it will have a negative effect on any efforts to try to practice this Presence. Who would want to be in the presence of a judgmental, angry, or punishing person, much less God?

Let us pray:
Most wondrous and glorious God show us how to undo all
the errors of the belief that you were less than Perfect Love.
Teach us how to be healed of the ignorance that keeps us
from the knowledge of who you truly are.

You have been revealed as a God of Peace and Justice;
a God who is our protector and our consoler and a God of
Unconditional Love. You are a God of over flowing joy. Help
us to discover and experience your true nature.

We thank you in advance for all you will teach us concerning
your love for us. Help us to learn the lessons of forgiveness
and peace that await us as we travel along this path of life.
Help us and heal us. We praise and adore you now and
forever. Amen.

Sickness and pain are calls for correction and change.
We must be willing to consider new ways of interpreting
what is going on inside us and around us for healing to
take place.

The fact that we even have an image of God is a limi-
tation. The First Commandment tells us not to make
images of God. This would include our making images
of God in our mind or even who we perceive God to be
according to what we have been taught.

However, in order to relate to the Divine, our minds
are such that we need something to visualize or imagine. This is acceptable as long as we do not take our
ideas of God too seriously and think that somehow our
image of God is beyond correction.

A story I heard recently made me smile. One day an
art teacher was teaching her third grade class to draw
whatever came into their minds. She wanted to see how
inventive they were and so she went about checking each

child. She came by little Sarah who was deeply absorbed in her artwork. She asked Sarah what she was drawing and Sarah responded that she was drawing God.

The Teacher replied "But no one knows what God looks like."

"Well," said Sarah, "they will now!"

We reveal by our words and actions the God we believe is the true God. If we believe in a God who is angry, then we will justify our anger. We justify our revenge and retaliation because we believe that is the way our image of God behaves. The question has to be asked whether our image of God has anything to do with the True God or is it just a projection of our needs.

Heal us 0 Lord. If we are to be truth seekers we need to be sincere in our quest to "know, love and serve God in this world," as the Catholic catechism puts it. C. S. Lewis tells us we must go beyond "mere religion" in our search for God. Formal religion tends to be too cultural, too ethnic and too institutional to give us an adequate image of God.

Contemplatives and mystics who have allowed the experience of God to touch them can be a source of knowledge. Mystics throughout the centuries have written of their experience with God. A God that is "beyond" or "other" than anything we ever imagined.

They know this through a direct experience of God's love.

Julian of Norwich was a mystic of the fourteenth century born in Norwich, England in 1342. During a serious illness at age thirty, Julian received sixteen dramatic revelations of the love of God. She wrote these revelations down and called them her "Showings." These revelations eventually led her to becoming what was then called an "Anchoress."

An anchoress was, in effect, a female hermit. She withdrew from society in order to devote herself completely to prayer and contemplation. Julian's counsel was sought by many people of her time. The following are some excerpts from her revelations.

*"And so I saw that God rejoices that he is our Father, and God rejoices that he is our Mother, and God rejoices that he is our true spouse, and that our soul is his beloved wife." (Showings, p.279)*

*"And so in all this contemplation it seemed to me that it was necessary to see and to know that we are sinners and commit many evil deeds which we ought to forsake, and leave many good deeds undone which we ought to do, so that we deserve pain, blame and wrath. And despite all this, I saw truly that Our Lord was never angry, and never will be.*

*"Because he is God, he is good, he is truth, he is love, he is peace; and his power, his wisdom, his charity and his unity do not allow him to be angry. For I saw truly that it is against the property of his power to be angry, and against the property of his wisdom and against the property of his goodness.*

*"God is that goodness which cannot be angry, for God is nothing but goodness. Our soul is united to him who is unchangeable goodness. And between God and our soul there is neither wrath nor forgiveness in his sight. For our soul is so wholly united to God, through his own goodness, that between God and our soul nothing can interpose." (Showings, p. 259)*

### Prayer of St. Teresa of Avila
Let nothing disturb you, nothing cause you fear; All things pass... Patience obtains all; Whoever has God needs nothing else, God alone suffices.

Somewhere in our religious upbringing we were given the impression that God's goodness to us depended on our being good or holy. If we committed a sin or, as I was led to believe, even had bad thoughts, then God looked on us with disdain and withheld goodness from us.

We were also led to believe that God was out there, somewhere up there looking down on us and judging all our thoughts and actions. A friend of mine told me that when she was a child and did something to upset her mother, her mother would look up to the ceiling in exasperation, raise her arms upwards, and complain to God, "Do you see what she's doing now God?"

My friend as a child thought that God lived on her mother's kitchen ceiling. How many times have we heard someone refer to God as "the man upstairs"?

We must develop a deeper understanding of God for our own peace of mind. Here is where healing is needed before we can begin to practice the Presence of God.

It involves de-programming our minds from the messages we received and retraining our minds towards a belief system of truth based on our experiences. A universal experience of God is not only possible but necessary if we are to discover for ourselves this "Presence."

Loving Lord God, awaken my understanding to the truth of who you are. Help me to experience your love. Amen.

What is important to remember is that any language we use about God is necessarily metaphorical. Even when Jesus calls God "Abba," that is, "Daddy," he is using an endearing term and saying that God is like a loving father.

Pope John Paul II wrote. *"God is our heavenly Father, but God is also a Mother to us."* God is far beyond what human language and symbols can express. Language must limit God to a person with a gender. Yet *"God is Spirit,"* (Jn. 4:24) and *"God is Love."* (I Jn 4:7)

Words and images may be helpful in trying to describe God, but they are always inadequate and can hamper our understanding of Divinity.

There are certain attributes of God that we can come to through reason, but we can only discover God through experience. We can experience God in quiet and stillness, when our personal needs and anxieties have been put aside.

God can be found in the beauty of nature, but beauty is found in the eye of the beholder as we have so often heard. God can be found in the love people have for one another, but human love falls short when compared to the unconditional love of God.

O Lord, help us to grasp the fullness of your wondrous love for us.

*"That is why I kneel before the Father from whom every family in heaven and on earth takes its name; and I pray that he will bestow on you gifts in keeping with the riches of his glory. May he strengthen you inwardly through the working of his Spirit. May Christ dwell in your hearts through faith, and may charity be the root and foundation of your life.*

*"Thus you will be able to grasp fully, with all the holy ones, the breadth and length and height and depth of Christ's love, and experience this love, which surpasses all knowledge so that you may attain to the fullness of God himself.*

*"To him whose power now at work in us can do immeasurably more than we ask or imagine... to him be glory in the church and in Christ Jesus through all generations, world without end. Amen." (Eph. 3:14-20)*

The search for God is like the search for the Holy Grail. We have this desire to seek and find it, but we keep looking outside ourselves for it. Yet, God cannot be found outside us for as Scripture teaches, *"In God we live and move and have our being." (Acts 17:28)*

It is not so much that God is in us rather that we are in God. If we practice contemplative prayer we will discover God at the center of our being rather than outside of ourselves. We then will have our own experience of God. Sooner or later this Love will reveal itself to us in a way that is unique to our soul. We will know longer have doubts about Divinity being with us and in us. From my experience I have found that the Love of God is always present and only waiting for our willing receptivity.

Let us pray:
O Loving Lord God I place myself before you seeking to experience your love. Help me to discover the Kingdom within. I want to know you and your way of peace, joy and love. Help me to live and move and have my being in you and you alone. Help me to no longer doubt but to understand. I want to live in the present moment knowing that you are with me, guiding and inspiring me in the ways of truth, beauty and harmony. I want to be one with you because there is where my contentment and my serenity lie. I belong to you O Lord. I have waited so long to know your love. I have hungered and thirsted for your loving Presence. Only in you is the emptiness removed and the fullness of life realized. I bless you and thank you for hearing the desire of my heart; to know, love, and serve you now and forever. Amen.

Father Peter McCall, the Franciscan Priest I worked with for many years, felt his calling was to be God's Public Relations Agent. Father Peter had a positive and loving relationship with God. He believed with all sincerity that God was Goodness personified.

A favorite slogan of his was, "There is nothing but

love in God." Father Peter also had a wonderful loving relationship with his own father who was old enough to be his grandfather by the time Peter was born.

Young Peter remembers growing up with approval and affection. His father showered him with love and encouragement, treating him always with respect. There was never a doubt in his mind that his father would do anything for him. It was easier for Father Peter to believe in a God of unconditional love than for many of us who had a very different, even negative, experience of a father.

My relationship with my father was completely the opposite of Father Peter's. Fortunately I was gifted with a grace that enabled me to see my father as a very sick man even before I knew alcoholism was recognized as a disease.

As a young child I somehow understood that my father did not know what he was really doing to himself and his family. This understanding however, did not stop me from being terrified of him. My father was a tough New York City mounted policeman who worked in the Harlem neighborhoods of New York City.

At times my father revealed his best self. He was a prolific self-taught artist, and enjoyed this gift and work of creating. When he was home on his day off he was usually at his easel. I was proud of his ability and of his oil paintings. He was even featured in the New York Times for his art work back in the late 1940s.

But we never knew when the volcano would erupt. There were guns in the house and although he kept them in a closet, we children were deathly frightened of him. We never knew what would set him off. My brothers and sisters and I felt at times our lives were in danger.

It was like living in a war zone, for when he was in a temper tantrum he physically tore the house apart in his madness. His strength was terrifying. When I was twelve I witnessed him in one of his rages, pick up the refrigerator, shake it and bounce it back down.

Given this background, there was no way that I could identify with God as Father, much less a loving father. Waves of fear would pass through me whenever God's will was mentioned. I imagined God's will to be harsh, judgmental, terrifying, and punishing.

The God I believed in was to be feared, not loved, for I never knew what awful calamity he might send if we did not obey his will. In retrospect I see how I had projected the fear of my own father towards the God of the Old and New Testaments.

The religious education I received during my childhood years taught me that God was only interested in how guilty I was. Naturally this led me to fear God the Father because of the punishment he would inflict. It was a religious nightmare.

I attended Catholic grade school and grew up with knowledge of Jesus Christ. My religious education also taught me that Jesus was someone who was approachable. We were taught to pray to Jesus and to his mother Mary.

Of course I only prayed to them when I was in trouble. I certainly did not live my life aware of their presence in my comings and goings. From what I had been taught Jesus was someone I could trust, for he was kind, loving, and gentle of heart and healed multitudes according to the Scriptures.

He was the Son of God, the Savior of the world. The religious practices we encountered as children were designed to instill in us faith and love for God. The downside of this education instilled in us the image of the suffering Christ.

We were taught that God's will was such that his only begotten son Jesus had to suffer a terrible tortuous death to save us from our sins. I grew up into adulthood with a terrible fear of the Father image of God. I often thought that I had to suffer in order to be in God's favor.

My heart would turn dark and a dread would cover me when I heard a priest or a nun speak about following God's will. I had been taught that one never knew what God's terrible will might be for us. Perhaps God's will was a lifetime of suffering and pain, or it could be sometimes God would give us a reprieve in between the suffering and pain. One never knew, though, what awful punishment he might send if we transgressed against his will.

This God I believed in kept me in a constant state of anxiety. In time I was to discover that the Powers of Heaven were not going to let me continue in my religious dysfunction, *"For nothing is impossible with God." (Luke 1:37)* Fortunately for all of us God is "The Hound of Heaven."

Let us pray:
O Loving Lord whenever I am confused or frightened I turn to you for reassurance. Rescue me from the terrors of my childhood. My soul longs to awaken and be enlightened so that I may no longer live in darkness. I yearn to be made whole and holy. I need your sweet love to heal me and your loving kindness to melt away my fears. I look to the Holy Spirit for guidance and a renewed purpose in my life. I want to leave behind all the confusion and disorder of the past and so I lay it down before you, Jesus ... at the foot of the cross. I want to live my life in peace and order and harmony. I want to be in your Presence, in your Light and bathed in your unconditional love. Thank you for this sacred stirring within my soul showing me the way to life as you would have me lead it. My only desire is to know and follow Your Holy Will to the best of my abilities. May your glory shine in me now and forever. Amen.

The Holy Spirit was with me and my mind was open enough to being taught some truths and so I began to learn about spiritual dimensions I never dreamed possible.

Some time after my spiritual awakening in 1973 I began to reflect on my fear of God as Father. Reasoning with myself, I began to understand the relationship Jesus had with God as Father.

In prayer I asked for help to clear up any distortions in my thinking. I attended a seminar where a Catholic preacher gave a teaching in which he compared the story of Abraham and Isaac with the sacrifice of Jesus on the cross.

Since this teaching disturbed me, I sought the advice of my friend, Father Peter McCall. He helped me to go over both accounts in the Bible and examine them for my own peace of mind. We both felt this particular preacher and others in the church were erring in regard to this bible story.

Chapter 22 of Genesis says that God put Abraham to the test in verse 2, God tells Abraham, *"Take your son, Isaac, your only one, whom you love, and you shall offer him up as a sacrifice on a height that I will show you."* Verse 6 continues, *"Thereupon Abraham took the wood for the sacrifice and laid it on his son Isaac's shoulders while he himself carried the fire and the knife."*

All this time, Isaac is completely unaware of his father's intentions and asks him of the whereabouts of the sacrificial lamb.

Abraham tells him that God will provide it. When they reach the top of the hill with Isaac still carrying the wood on his shoulders, his father subdues him, ties him up, and places him on the altar of sacrifice.

At this moment, though, God has a change of heart and tells Abraham to spare the boy. The preacher was using this story as an analogy to explain God giving up his only son as a sacrifice on the cross. I could not understand how this story of Abraham and Isaac could be taught as an analogy in order to understand the passion and death of Jesus.

I questioned how anyone could love a God who would demand that a father (Abraham) turn over his only son to be burned and put to death for some sort of test. No wonder my heart shrank with fear at the thought of such a terrifying God.

Father Peter pointed out to me that when the Book of Genesis was written, people were primitive and this story is intended to be directed against the practice of human sacrifice, which at the time was common among the pagans.

What an 'ah-ha' moment this was for me! Once we realize that this was the primary purpose of the story, we see that it has no relationship to the story of Jesus. There are other contradictions as well.

Isaac was just a boy and totally ignorant of what his father was about to do. Jesus was an adult who knew that once he preached a gospel of peace, it was possible that violent men would put him to death. It had happened to prophets before him.

Let us pray:
O Divine Wisdom, We pray for the grace of enlightenment. Teach us 0 Lord.
Deliver us from the fault of ignorance, and from the limitations of this world. You are drawing us into an ever expanding awareness and knowledge of you. Your thoughts are not our thoughts 0 Lord. We need to be guided by The Holy Spirit in order to learn, and discover a greater understanding of you, of ourselves and others. Lead us on and enlighten us. You alone have the words of eternal life. Amen.

In the book of the prophet Hosea, God clearly states, *"For it is love I desire, not sacrifice, and the knowledge of God rather than holocausts." (6:6)* Jesus himself refers to this teaching when he tells the people, *"Go and learn the meaning of the words, 'It is mercy I desire and not sacrifice'." (Mt. 9:13)*

The Scriptures tell us that Jesus had foreknowledge of his impending death. He even predicts it. *"He was teaching his disciples in this vein: 'The Son of Man is going to be delivered into the hands of men who will put him to death; three days after his death he will rise'."(Mark 9:31-33)* Jesus was a man very much in command of his mission and destiny.

Jesus was not a victim! He chose to be obedient even unto death (Re: Phil. 2:8), not to appease a wrathful God, but to show that he could still be master over fear and violence.

He chose to die at the hands of violent men to show that violence, hatred and evil could not separate him from the peace and love of his Father. (Re: Rom. 8:35-39)

The Gospel of Mark states, *"The Centurion who stood guard over him, upon seeing the manner of his death, declared, 'Clearly this was the Son of God!'"(16:13)*

Why did the centurion say this? What was so different about the death of Jesus and all others who had been crucified? The Romans had used crucifixion as a way of terrorizing the Jews, and thousands had been put to death by this means.

I believe this particular centurion was given a deep spiritual insight in that he saw Jesus in all his glory as the Prince of Peace and the Son of the Living God. Jesus the Christ, the Holy one, was able to see through those who hated him and still have mercy on them.

His obedience to God was in his ultimate willingness to show that the way to Heaven is through the grace of forgiveness. We can see the glorious victory of Christ when he cried out from the cross on Calvary, *"Father, for-give them; they do not know what they are doing!"(Luke 23:34)*

I began to receive more clarity after reading from Chapter 14 of the Gospel of John. In this passage of Scripture Jesus is talking to his disciple Philip, saying *"If you really knew me, you would know my Father also."* *(Jn. 14)*

Philip replies to Jesus, *"Show us the Father and that will be enough for us."*

*"Philip,"* Jesus replied, *"After I have been with you all this time, you still do not know me? Whoever has seen me has seen the Father. How can you say 'Show us the Father?' Do you not believe that I am in the Father and the Father is in me? The words I speak are not spoken of me; it is the Father who lives in me accomplishing his works. Believe me that I am in the Father and the Father is in me, or else believe because of the works I do."*

This conversation Jesus had with Philip was thought-provoking, and I came to the decision that in order to have a healthy frame of mind I needed to be healed of my underlying fear of God. Upon reflection I received the understanding that Jesus was in God and God was in Jesus. They were one! There was no separation! And the Kingdom of God was within me where the Christ light dwelled! Oh, how I needed to be healed from the night-mare of my childhood.

Thank you for hearing my prayer and answering me Loving Lord, God.

As a result of this shift in my thinking, an amazing thing began to happen to me. I began receiving mes-sages in my mind, that is, words of affirmation to help me de-program my fear of God as Father.

It simply came to me one day as an idea. I know now

it was The Holy Spirit guiding me in a way I could comprehend. Under this guidance I began to re-program myself, repeating words and phrases over and over again that were positive statements about God and me.

It was a childish way of doing it, but at that time I was so new in the ways of spirituality. I took time out to learn to be quiet. In the silence I would listen and repeat to myself what I heard and it went like this: "I am a precious person created by a most wonderful loving Creator. I am a precious gift created by a most wonderful and loving God. I am infinitely loved by God. I am a loveable child of God." I would repeat this exercise in various ways.

I do not deny that what happened to me as a child was real. But this mode of healing defused the negative power that the fear of God had over me. It wasn't until a long time later that I discovered affirmations were used in various healing systems; at the time I did not know that and I was being shown a way that would work for me.

Affirmations are used as a declaration of Truth. *"You will know the Truth and the truth will set you free." (Jn. 8:32)* Just as we were created by the spoken word of God, (Re: Gn. 1:36), so the words we speak have creative power.

*"So shall my word be that goes forth from my mouth; it shall not return to me void, but shall do my will, achieving the end for which I sent it." (Is. 55:11)*

In a similar manner, our words of affirmation and truth bring about what they decree. Just as all thoughts are powerful, the words which represent these thoughts are powerful.

I have discovered over time through personal experience, that God is ultimate Goodness, Perfect Unconditional Love, and Overflowing Joy! I have also come to believe that God is not the source of sickness or natural disasters. While we are on this journey of discovery, God has made available to us ways of knowing... if we would just stop, be still, and listen.

Whenever I would get stuck in a negative frame of mind I would practice these principles and begin to affirm the truth. "God is Love and I am God's beloved child." As we repeat the words over and over again, our unconscious picks it up and eventually we begin to believe what we are saying because they are truth statements.

"God is so good. God is so good to me. God's watchful gaze protects me, I am safe. Thank you God for loving me so dearly."

Many miracles opened up for me at the time so I know this is a system that works. For those who would like to be set free from their fears, saying these affirmations can be a major source of healing.

*"Only goodness and kindness shall follow me all the days of my life." (Psalm 23)*

This is a wonderfully healing affirmation.

When I look back at my early years, my sense of self -esteem was in desperate need of healing. I felt a deep wound, an abyss in the core of my being, a hole in my soul. I was willing to try whatever would work for me.

The more we become conscious of who we really are the more awake we become to the truth of our being. We are spiritual beings infinitely loved by a benevolent God. Yes. So much is mystery!

The challenge is to discover our true selves as the mystery of our lives unravel. St. Theresa of Avila once wrote that it is not so much our working at getting to heaven, rather; it is heaven all the way.

*Let our prayer be, "Lord help me to experience Heaven all the way to Heaven. Amen."*

*"And I shall dwell in the house of the Lord for years to come." (Psalm 23:8)*

The Psalms are a great source of help in affirming oneself. All one has to do is personalize them. Many of the Psalms are already personalized. You just have to believe the words were meant for you in particular.

For example, Psalm 27 reads, *"The Lord is my light and my salvation; whom should I fear? The Lord is my life's refuge of whom should I be afraid?"*

Repeating this as an affirmation over and over again can assuage any fears we may be experiencing.

As my spiritual journey continued, it was revealed to me that it is not enough to believe in God as good and to believe that God is Love. The Book of Genesis in the Old Testament tells us that God created us in his Image and likeness.

*"God looked at everything he had made, and he found it very good." (Gen. 1:31)*

The words of Jesus found in the Gospels of John and Matthew confirms the passage in Genesis. *"Jesus spoke to them once again: 'I am the light of the world, no follower of mine shall ever walk in darkness; no, he shall possess the light of life'." (Jn. 8:12)*

In Matthew, Jesus says: *"You are the light of the world. A city set on a hill cannot be hidden; men do not light a lamp and then put it under a bushel basket. They set it on a stand where it gives light to all in the house. In the same way your light must shine before all so that they may see the goodness in your acts and give praise to your heavenly Father." (Mt. 5:14-16)*

We are instructed to use these metaphors to affirm the truth about ourselves. We need to free ourselves from the limitations of the false-self system that is the self that we created to survive this world up to now.

In order to understand our true selves we need to understand the nature of God. We cannot put God in a box once we begin to awaken to the truth. The truth is that God does not give light. God is light! God does not give love. God is Love! God is Life! God's life is present in us! God is eternal life! Our Christian faith believes we will live eternally, that is, forever in the afterlife. We affirm this truth when we say to ourselves;" I am the light of the world."

Since we are not separated from the God of Light and Love and Life we can affirm these truths about ourselves. The following is a prayer form of affirmations proclaiming our identification with the Lord.

Take time out to be still, sitting or lying in a comfortable position and begin by repeating the following positive statements to yourself at least three times each.

- God is so good...and so am I.
- God is Love...and so am I.
- The Lord is the light of the world... I am the light of the world!
- God is Holy...I am holy.
- God is Wisdom...I am wise.
- God is Joy...I am joyful.
- God Understands... I understand.
- Where I am, God is... where God is I am.
- God is Creator...I am creative.

Continue with your own affirmations.


Perhaps in time, after maturing in the spiritual life, that is; understanding God's true nature as well as our own true nature, we may lay aside affirmations. We may be able to become conscious enough to know the truth of who we are. "You will know the truth and the truth will set you free."

At this stage of my spiritual journey I do not need to depend on affirmations to help me in times of darkness. At these times I return to contemplative prayer. However it was this mode of prayer using affirmations that opened the doors for me to experience emotional and spiritual freedom from my many fears about God as Father.

Other people who want to change their image of God may find it helpful too.

Let us pray:
Loving Lord God, I am embarking on a path of spiritual discovery. I need all the guidance you can give me. Help me to accept myself as I truly am. Help me to die to the false self, the self I created in order to survive this world. I am at a crossroads where I need to make the right decisions concerning the path that leads me to discover my True Self. I need to see through the deceptions of this world so that I may be clear about who you are and who I am. Grant me a clear and sound mind that I may think rightly. I have many fears 0 Lord that have to do with my ideas of who you are, fears that haunt my perceptions of a Father image. Prepare my mind to receive the truth about who you really are. I have a deep desire to be taught and to know and to understand so that I may be set free from fear of the unknown. Lord, I am learning that you are closer to me than the breath I breathe. Grant to me the grace of humility. The grace to let go of all preconceived notions of who I think you are. Grant to me teachable moments, for you are the intelligence that guides me. You know my needs even before I ask for them. Help me to forgive myself for all my mistakes and erring ways. Show me how to obtain the Kingdom within, where you dwell. Be with me in all my comings and goings. I want to know the truth and you are the only one who can show me the path to that truth. I need your love, I need your peace, and I need to be set free. You are eternal life and all goodness of life flows from you. I yearn for knowledge of you. I yearn to be in your Presence. I yearn to live and move and have my being in you and you alone. Thank you for satisfying my longing, for you, 0 Lord God. You are the Holy One I seek with all my heart. Never let me think that I can be

separated from you ever again. Blessed be your holy name now and forever. Amen and Amen!

Chapter 5

## The Strength and Power of Personal prayer

## Using Psalms, Proverbs, and Other Scripture with Original Prayers.

*"When you are praying, do not behave like the hypocrites who love to stand and pray in synagogues or on street corners in order to be noticed. I give you my word, they are already repaid. Whenever you pray, go to your room, close your door, and pray to your Father in private.*

*"Then your Father, who sees what no one sees, will repay you. In your prayer do not rattle on like the pagans. They think they will win a hearing by the sheer multiplication of words. Do not imitate them. Your Father knows what you need before you ask him."(Mt. 6:5-9)*

The spiritual path calls us to be in conscious union with God through prayer and we are also called to pray for one another. Saint Paul urges us, *"With all prayer and supplication, pray at every moment in the Spirit. Pray for me, that speech may be given me to open my mouth to make known with boldness the mystery of the gospel. (Eph. 6:19)*

When we include the power of prayer in our lives, we

can live each day more fully awake and alive, consciously with our eyes wide open.

> Let us pray:
> Loving Lord God we thank you for the gift of faith. Help us
> to be aware of your loving presence today. This day, is a
> day that has never been lived before, a brand new day to
> make healthy choices through the power of prayer making
> us aware of your presence. With the help of the Holy Spirit
> may everything we say, and do this day, be guided and in-
> spired in the holy name of Jesus. Help us to live well this
> day, remembering you have promised to be with us. You
> alone are the holy one, the Lord, the Lamb of God. We thank
> you and praise you now and forever. Amen!

As we develop the habit of prayer it is inevitable that we
will change. I used to pray that others in my life would
change. It was a hard lesson for me to find out that it
was I who needed changing.

The gradual changes that came about were hardly
even noticeable to me. Only after some time of being
faithful to the daily practice of prayer did I begin to see
the shift in my disposition and attitude.

For example, a woman I knew aggravated me because of her loudness and her eagerness to gossip. At
first I gave her the benefit of the doubt and chalked it up
to the fact that I did not know her very well. After some
time, though, I realized I had begun to avoid this person
whenever the occasion arose.

It annoyed me to no end, for it seemed that I was constantly running into her. I knew my attitude toward her
was not doing me any good but I felt helpless to do anything about it. To top it off, one of my children and one
of her children didn't much care for each other either.

At one point there was an unfortunate encounter between them, and this woman called me to complain. Of course I fussed and fumed to whoever would listen. I was downright furious.

Eventually I calmed down, took time to think about it, and decided to bring the situation to prayer. In my prayer I asked for a peaceful solution and that I might also perceive this woman differently. I left it at that and for quite awhile I didn't see her, for which I was grateful.

When I chanced to meet her again, it was in a group setting. I realized after some moments of chatting that I actually enjoyed her company. I noticed that she had a sense of humor. In the course of our conversation, I discovered that she had a sincere love for children and had a seemingly generous and compassionate nature.

I left her that day marveling at the miracle God had done in changing me and my perception. As Scripture says, *"Rejoice in hope, be patient under trial, persevere in prayer (Rom. 12:12)*

Holy Spirit you are a most wondrous helper and counselor. I thank you for helping me change my perception so that I may see those around me through your loving eyes. Amen.

## Jesus is the Light of the World

For many years I had been afraid of the dark and would keep the light on at night. Once I was tossing and turning in bed so I decided to go into the den that I used as a prayer room. I sat in the dark and prayed silently. In the darkness I saw flecks of light similar to dust particles that we see in the light of day.

I was given an insight that the light of Christ is present even in the darkness. At first I was stunned and thought that I must be imagining this. Opening and closing my eyes any number of times, I tried to see if what I was seeing would still be there. The flecks of light remained and I finally accepted the experience as an awesome gift from God.

I was so excited by this revelation and began to lose my fear of the darkness within me along with the dark of the night. *"The light shines on in the darkness, a darkness that did not overcome it." (Jn. 1:5)*

A remarkable slogan was given to me at that time: "Fear is the dark room where negatives are developed."

Let us pray:
Loving Lord God, you are the fullness and radiance of all light. We ask and pray that your protection be with us throughout the night. Protect us from our innermost fears and concerns. We ask to be set free from the root cause of the fear of the dark and of the night. Come shower us with your graces and heal our childhood terrors. You alone are the light of our souls and of our minds. Shine your light upon us as we trust you to keep watch over us. Assign your holy angels to stand guard over us throughout the night. Thank you dearest Savior for hearing our cry of distress. Blessed be your holy light. Amen.
Blessed be the name of Our Lord and Savior Jesus Christ now and forever. Amen.

As my spiritual life developed, I fashioned the routine of rising early each morning to begin my day in prayer. This would take the form of some sort of spiritual reading followed by Scripture and then usually interceding in prayer for various family members and friends.

As a Roman Catholic I began attending daily Mass after I sent my children off to school. Eventually I learned various forms of contemplative prayer and would practice incorporating them into my established routine. On one such morning as I was deep in silent prayer I heard an inner voice speak to me.

The words came to me directly and clearly within my

mind. I heard, *"Fear will no longer have power over you."* This didn't seem possible to me. Of course I pondered over this and wondered about it. After some reflection I finally came to understand that I would no doubt have many fears in the future. The assurance of the words spoken however, gave me confidence that my fears would eventually abate with the awareness that I was protected by God's loving presence.

There have been many occasions when I encountered real and imagined fears since that time. There were also times when there were confrontations with evil, yet to my happy surprise and relief they have always somehow been alleviated. *"The Lord is my light and my salvation; whom should I fear?" (Psalm 27:1)*

The following story is an example of an encounter with evil.

A chapel where Father Peter and I held services was located in an area of the city that was older and rundown. One afternoon when I pulled up in my car to park I noticed a man shouting at a woman who was holding a baby girl in her arms.

The woman was young, perhaps in her twenties, and she was crying. The man had her backed up against the fieldstone monastery wall and kept gesturing menacingly at her. I thought better of leaving my car and began to pray for help.

In the meantime a couple of elderly people standing across the street in front of an apartment house watched, looking alarmed. I prayed that a police car would suddenly and miraculously appear. But none did. I thought perhaps I should run past the couple very quickly, up the stairs into the church and get the priest to come out and rescue the woman and baby.

At this point it seemed to be my only option. Meanwhile the man was becoming more agitated and I was afraid he was going to strike the woman. I cautiously got out of my car and began to tiptoe past them on the street, avoiding the sidewalk they were on.

Suddenly, to my own surprise, I stopped dead in my tracks, turned to the man, and spoke in a very bold and authoritative tone, "Leave that woman and baby alone, you are abusing them!"

Much to my astonishment the man turned to me and said, "What?"

I repeated my message just as boldly, "Leave that woman and baby alone, you are abusing them!"

He looked at me long and hard, turned to the baby and with a Cheshire cat smile, patted the baby on top of the head, said something to the woman quietly, and immediately left in his car.

I was frozen in disbelief and began shaking like a leaf. After seeing that the woman and child were okay I offered them sanctuary in the chapel, which she turned down. She apparently had her own car up the street and left in it.

I went inside the chapel and related the story to Father Peter. Of course when Father Peter found out that he had been my first instinct as rescuer, he offered me a "thanks-a-lot" tone of voice half in jest, half in earnest.

In hindsight I can't help but believe I was set up by The Holy Spirit revealing the authenticity of the words spoken to me in the past, that is, that "fear would no longer have power over me." Wisdom instructs me to pray only to know the will of God and for the power to do it.

"Help" is the only authentic prayer we ever really need to say. Praise God from whom all blessings flow!

I began to have longer periods of inner peace and serenity. The transformation was ever so subtle and came about over an extended period of time. How enormously grateful I am to our loving Lord for providing a solution to my dilemma.

I had been in a desperate frame of mind for far too

long and now I was becoming more aware and freer in spirit than I had ever thought possible. *"It was for liberty that Christ has set us free." (Gal 5:1)*

Let us pray:
O loving Lord God I give you great honor and praise for your Loving kindness. I acknowledge you are my Savior, my Redeemer as I turn to you in my time of need. May your healing light shine on the darkness of my fears, my worries, and my anxieties I affirm and acknowledge that you have promised to be with me always. I am safe and free. I am no longer in danger for you have promised to remain with me always .I thank you for the gift of my watchful guardian angels. Holy Spirit come to my assistance and help me to remember that you are always there when I need help. I am sustained and supported by a Divine Light. I am reminded that God is perfect Love... I am God's beloved... God's unconditional love is with me now and every moment of my existence. I thank you for your great goodness. I place my trust in knowing you are ever present to me, constantly watching over me. Blessed be the holy name of the Lord! I Praise you now and forever. .Amen.

## Security under God's Protection
*"You who dwell in the shelter of the Most High,*
*    Who abide in the shadow of the Almighty, Say to the Lord, "My refuge and my fortress,*
*    My God in whom I trust.*
*    For He will rescue you from the snare of the fowler, from the destroying pestilence*
*    With his pinions he will cover you,*
*    And under his wings you shall take refuge; His faithfulness is a buckler and a shield.*
*    You shall not fear the terror of the night nor the arrow that flies by day*
*    Not the pestilence that roams in darkness Nor the dev-*

*astating plague at noon.*

*Though a thousand fall at your right side, near you it shall not come.*

*Rather with your eyes shall you behold and see the requital of the wicked,*

*Because you have the Lord for your refuge; You have made the most high your stronghold." (Psalm 91)*

It is not always easy to embrace a loving concept of God because so many of us have been wounded by just plain lack of love and kindness by the negative elements that make up this society.

In my experience of praying with people and in my own process of healing, I have found that it takes a while to get accustomed to the kind of unconditional love that Jesus has to offer. When Jesus walked on this earth, he must have exuded an amazingly powerful energy of unconditional love. The gospel narratives tell us how crowds flocked to his demonstrations of magnetic goodness.

We are still flocking to Him two thousand years later. In scripture, we read, *"He cured all who were afflicted."* (Mt. 8:16) Again, we read, *"After sunset they brought him all who were ill. Before long the whole town was gathering outside the door. Those whom he cured who were variously afflicted were many." (Mark: 32-34)*

Jesus often instructed those he cured that their faith made them well. The story of the centurion's servant illustrates this:

*"...as Jesus entered Capernaum, a centurion approached him with this request, 'Sir, my serving boy is at home in bed paralyzed, suffering painfully.'*

*He said to him, 'I will come and cure him.'*

*'Sir,' the centurion said in reply, 'I am not worthy to have you under my roof. Just give an order and my boy*

*will get better. I am a man under authority myself and I have troops assigned to me. If I give one man the order, 'Dismissed,' off he goes. If I say to another, 'Come here,' he comes. If I tell my slave, 'Do this,' he does it.*

*"Jesus showed amazement on hearing this and remarked to his followers, 'I assure you I have never found this much faith in Israel.' To the centurion Jesus said, 'Go home, it shall be done because you trusted.' That very moment the boy got better." (Mt. 8:5-13)*

Many years ago when we first began the healing prayer ministry in New York we received a phone call from a young man. We had prayed with him in the past for a serious illness, and he had gotten well.

Father Peter took the phone call and heard this young man say; "Father Peter, if you and Maryanne pray with me I will get well again."

Father Peter was so amazed by this young man's faith in our prayers for him that he spoke about it often through the years. Yes, we did pray with him and he was cured. Praise God!

On another occasion described in the Gospel of Matthew, two blind men came after Jesus crying out, *"Son of David, have pity on us!"*

*When he got to the house, the blind men caught up with him. Jesus said to them, "Are you confident I can do this?"*

*"Yes, Lord," they told him. At that he touched their eyes and said, "Because of your faith it shall be done to you", 'and they recovered their sight." (Mt. 9: 27-30)*

Faith is confident assurance concerning what we hope for, and conviction about things we do not see. (Re: Heb. 11:1) Faith is one of the fruits of the power and strength of personal prayer and produces joy, hope, peace, and love. A wonderful freedom occurs when we allow our faith to take us into the infinite knowledge of the sweetness and joy of God's perfect love.

Early in my walk in faith I realized that I did not know how to have fun in my life. I felt guilty if I allowed myself simple pleasures. A friend bought us tickets to the circus and instead of enjoying the circus I felt a total lack of joy. I even felt guilty being there, for some unknown dark reason.

I realized I didn't even know how to enjoy myself. I remember praying silently, asking The Holy Spirit to show me how to enjoy the show. My growing up years had been filled with too many joyless happenings, crisis and disappointments so I had no foundation to base joy or happiness upon.

Of course I knew I needed healing. In praying for help I asked God for newfound joy in my life. I have some recollections of being a happy little girl and vaguely remember some people asking me questions and whatever I said to them apparently charmed them for I remember clearly being delighted by their joyful reaction.

It is not my intention to denigrate the family I grew up in but the truth was that there was absolutely no joy in the lives of the adults and therefore they didn't even know how to express it to us children.

The emotions that were expressed the most were of rigid control and rage. These harsh conditions gradually suppressed that magical little girl. As I grew older humiliation was heaped upon my spirit. My earlier sensitive, joyful nature became squelched, fearful and depressed. The atmosphere was unforgiving, puritanical and dominating control giving rise to bouts of terror.

Early on in my spiritual journey I attended a Christian Healing Conference. The keynote speaker, a priest, was addressing the issues of childhood emotional wounds and the lack of healing which simply was not available in our churches at the time.

He proclaimed most emotionally and powerfully, "We were robbed! We were robbed!" I'll never forget thinking that's exactly what happened to us as children, (and to countless others, as I've discovered).

We were robbed of the precious gift of innocence and happiness. I suffered terribly for many years. Thankfully the Lord offered me a way out of my suffering, giving me hope and encouragement. Trusting the Lord to teach me how to enjoy life became an exciting venture.

Jesus speaks of this in the Gospel of John, *"The thief comes only to steal and slaughter and destroy, I came that they might have Life and have it to the full!"* (Jn. 10:10)

*"You will show me the path to life, fullness of joys in your presence, the delights of your right hand forever."* (Psalm 16:11)

As God would have it, I broke out of the mold I was expected to live in, and during the years of spiritual growth I sprang forth like a budding plant in springtime. The Lord knew my soul and was aware I was thirsting and hungering for life in all its abundance.

I was to be given many opportunities to enjoy life. As I opened myself to the joy of these experiences, it became easier for me to delight in them. Thanks to the ministry of healing I was able to travel to many different countries in Europe, Canada, and Mexico and to places far and wide in this country as well.

At other times various friends would treat me to Broadway musicals and to various and interesting restaurants in Manhattan. I saw it all as a gift from God in showing me how to enjoy this life.

At one point in our ministry Father Peter and I decided to give four-day retreats. Healing retreats required that we touch on pretty tough subjects involving physical, spiritual, emotional, generational and environmental healing.

A typical retreat given usually at a Retreat House would start on a Friday evening and end at noon on Sunday. We decided to incorporate a funny skit on Saturday night which meant we had to add another day to include all the topics involving the healing program schedule.

Usually the theme of the skit would spoof whatever we were teaching on that weekend. We felt we needed to balance the serious retreat with humor and fun. As a result we formed a clown ministry. It sometimes involved renting costumes, and some of the skits were so original and outrageously funny we would roll with laughter. It was clear to us that the work was so hilarious that only a great joy of the Lord could have created it through the minds and spirits of those participating.

I look back at those times with great fondness for the fun and good humor and hilarity. Laughter is good medicine! *"A glad heart lights up the face, but by mental anguish the spirit is broken," (Prv. 15:13) "A merry heart is the health of the body, but a depressed spirit dries up the bones." (Prv. 17:22)*

Joy is and always will be a top spiritual gift in the Kingdom of God as far as I am concerned.

Let us pray:
0 Loving Lord God, create within my heart and soul the joy of living. Stir up within me a new zeal for passion and devotion to life. I want to sing and dance and be happy. Teach me how to be playful. Dear Jesus, show me how to laugh and be merry. Teach me how to delight in the ways you show me your love. I want to leave behind me all my sorrows and pain. In this present moment you abide with me in spirit and in truth and joy. May I be granted the mind of Christ that I too may know the love and peace that only you can give. May my life reflect the image of goodness you have created within me. I sing a song of gratitude for all the gifts, blessings

and treasures you have graced me with. May I draw ever closer to you, 0 sweet, gentle Lord. I yearn to be one with you. God of my heart and soul I am humbled to be in your holy presence. You have filled my life with sweetness where once there was bitterness. You have restored my soul and set me free to wander freely in the fields of hope for a better life here and in the forever. May my every breath proclaim you as the Lord of my being. I rejoice in the knowledge that I am your beloved child and you are beloved of my soul. I am in you and you are in me. Fill me with joy that I may truly be in union with you, Jesus and the Holy Spirit and, all the angels and saints. May the joy of Jesus be my strength. May every fiber of my being proclaim the joy and wonder of knowing God's infinite love. Blessed be the Lord God of life, holiness, peace and love. Blessed be the name of Jesus now and forever. Amen.

There is no right or wrong way to pray. As I mentioned before the most honest prayer we can say is "help." All we do is to ask for the help of the Holy Spirit every time we pray. As to whether or not our prayers should be specific or general, we should feel comfortable with whatever form of prayer we feel is inspired. We pray as we can, not as we ought.

The following prayers are based on the belief that the greatest area in which we need God's help is forgiveness. Forgiveness means the ability to see people and circumstances through the eyes of the Holy Spirit, who alone can teach forgiveness. All authentic prayer will express a desire to see the world around us through the eyes of the Holy Spirit, or through Christ's vision. *"We have the mind of Christ." (1 Cor. 2:16)*

We need the help of the Holy Spirit to undo the past. We need it to accept the Holy Spirit's present interpretation of what we are experiencing. All we can do is ask

the Holy Spirit to remove the blocks to the awareness of
love.

Come Holy Spirit...enlighten me, guide me, strengthen me
and console me. Amen.

In prayer we simply become more aware of the presence
of the Holy Spirit. He is the one who prays for us and
with us. It is the prayer of the Holy Spirit which is all
powerful. We believe that all prayer is already answered,
because the Answer, the Holy Spirit, has already been
given.

The more we grow in the awareness of God's presence
within us, the more we grow in prayer.

The least important part of prayer is what we say
to God. The most important part of prayer is what God
says to us. In this sense, all authentic prayer is contemplative rather than active.

For this reason, we include both talking prayer and
listening prayer in this section.

I hope that these prayers help you grow in the awareness of God's unconditional love. If the words that have
been written get in the way of the Holy Spirit, forget the
words and just listen to the Divine.

The following prayers were composed by my beloved
friend and cofounder of The House of Peace, Inc., Father
Peter McCall, Franciscan, Capuchin Priest. I include
them here as a tribute to his memory.

Healing Prayers for Everyday
By Father Peter McCall, OFM, Cap.

Holy Spirit, help me to begin this day with a greater
awareness of your presence within me. Help me to know
that I am never alone and that you go with me wherever
I go. Help me to realize that you can no more abandon

me than you can any part of your creation. Help me to know my oneness with God and all creation.

Help me to accept today as a gift from God, a chance to choose again. Help me to see that the past is gone, that it has faded away into nothingness, and that it need not have any power over me.

Holy Spirit, help me to undo the past by accepting this holy moment of release. It is your gift to me. I want to accept it and join myself with all creation in choosing God's plan for my redemption. Help me not to substitute my own plan, but allow you to teach me and lead me through the circumstances of this day. Help me to learn and teach the lessons of forgiveness with every person who comes my way today,

Holy Spirit, help me realize that only today is real and now is the moment of my salvation. Help me to heal and be healed as I join with all who come my way today and acknowledge your presence in both of us.

Help me to be attentive to your voice and to give you my little willingness to listen and obey. I give this day to you because you have given it to me. Help me to witness to your love and peace as I leave behind all guilt and fear.

Holy Spirit, help me to be truly helpful. Help me to represent THE ONE who sent me. Help me not to worry about what to say or how to say it. Help me to trust that THE ONE who sent me will direct and guide me. Help me to realize that my happiness this day lies only in doing your will.

Holy Spirit, help me to see with loving eyes today!
Help me to hear with loving ears!
Help me to touch with loving hands!
Help me to speak with a loving voice!
Help me to be your healing presence today!

Holy Spirit, help me to be aware of who I really am,

a beloved child of God. Help me to never doubt my gifts, but use them for the benefit of all creation. Help me to share my gifts with each person who comes my way. Help me to look lovingly on this present moment, because it is only here that I can meet you. I thank you for the beauty in every person I meet this day. Every person who comes my way is your gift to me. Help me to look on them and to see your presence in them.

Holy Spirit, I invite you to lead my way today. You alone know the way. You are my Advocate, my guide sent from Good You speak for my true self. Help me to hear only what you have to say. You are in charge of my salvation. Lead me, and help me to follow you.

Holy Spirit, help me to accept your judgment of every person I meet this day. You know all things about everybody, and you see them as not guilty. Help me to share this verdict, because it is the same with which I judge myself. You send every person I meet today. They are all my teachers. I accept the gift of each relationship. Help me to make each relationship holy because this is your will.

Holy Spirit, help me to be brother or sister to all who come my way today. Help me to see equality and friendship in all people I meet. Help me never to use another person for my own advantage or attach the sanctity you have placed within him or her.

Holy Spirit, help me to give you all my thoughts which would destroy my peace. I exchange all unholy feelings for your holy interpretations. Only the truth will set me free. Teach me the truth about myself, God, and others. I place my mind under your guidance and place my body at your service. Only you know what is beneficial for me. Help me to hear your voice and to experience your healing.

## Listening Prayer to God

My child, do not be afraid I have redeemed you and called you by name. I am always with you. I have given you a destiny, a sacred function to perform. I have given you the power to experience my peace and to extend it to others.

My child, my peace is always with you wherever you go. You can forget it, but you cannot lose it. You are always precious in my eyes, and I love you. Love yourself today as I love you. Don't be so hard on yourself. I am in charge of your salvation, not you. Don't take yourself so seriously. You did not choose me. It was I who chose you. All you need do is be still and listen to my voice.

My child, I am always with you to protect you and to watch over you. Put your trust in me, and you will never be harmed. Trust me as I trust you. Believe in me as I believe in you. I want you laugh and smile more, because your salvation is already assured soften the brow of your face. There is no condemnation for those who believe in my mercy.

My child, let go of any fear of success or failure today. Each beat of your heart is a new creation, and I will always renew and refresh you. It is my will that you enjoy yourself today. Once you place this day in my hands, you can relax and be assured of my constant attention. I guarantee that I will never leave you alone.

## Talking To God

Loving Lord God, Your Grace is given me today. I claim it now. You created me wonderfully in your own image and Likeness. I am the child you love. By your Grace I live. By your Grace I am released by your Grace I give and receive all I need today to heal and be healed Help me to be more aware of who I truly am, your child. Help me never to doubt my true identity in you, but to share it with all living things in harmony.

Loving Lord God, help me to remember you today. This is all I want; this is all I need. You alone are holy, and my holiness is a sharing in your life. Help me never to believe that I am separated from you, but help me to accept my true reality. Help me to receive what you have already given, and help me to realize that our minds are joined now as they will be throughout all eternity.

Loving Lord God, I have no words to give you. I would but listen to your word. Lead me today as a Father leads a little child along the way he does not understand. I will follow, sure and safe, because I know that your Spirit leads the way. If I stumble, you will raise me up again. If I forget the way, you will remind me. If I wander off, you will call me back again. Help me to walk with You today.

## Calling on Jesus

Jesus, my brother, help me to see today as you see. Though you are hidden behind the disguise of the unattractive, the demanding, and the unreasonable, help me to recognize you and say, "Jesus, my brother, how good it is for us to be here." I will be healed as I share with those who come my way the good news of your presence in both of us.

## Listening to Jesus

My child, I need your voice today. I need your hands and feet. I need your eyes to look upon and bless our tired brothers and sisters who are weary of the world they see and believe there is nothing more. How can I teach them except though you? How can I give hope but through your words? How can you hear me except through them?

My child, I have chosen you as an instrument of my peace. To whomever I send you, you shall go. Whatever I command you to speak, you shall spear Do not worry or be afraid. I will place my words in your mouth. He, who hears you, hears me. He, who sees you, sees me.

My child be easy on yourself today. It is my will that my brothers and sisters be happy and be of good cheer. It is I who send you, so it is I who empower you to accomplish all I have in mind. The Spirit of the Living God will speak through you. Act and speak in unison with me. Do not be afraid; I have overcome the world.

## Prayer for Continuous Healing

Loving Lord God, I am your child; I come into Your presence now to accept the gifts of healing which You have already given. I rest in Your presence and forget for just a moment my problems and my pain. I quiet my mind so as to be more receptive to your love.

I focus my attention on Your presence within me and forget myself for just an instant. It is in stillness that I hear Your voice of love and healing. Help me to be still and know that you are my God. In quiet and in confidence will my strength and health return.

Loving Lord God, with the help of Jesus and his Spirit I now make a decision to let go of any bitterness, unforgiveness, or anger in my being. Even if I do not emotionally feel this way, I stand on my decision to choose love in place of fear, peace in place of conflict

Loving Lord God, into Your hands I commit my spirit, mind, and body. Whatever hurt, guilt or darkness I feel within myself, I place in the light of Your presence.

Gently remove forever whatever is harmful or destructive within my being. I enter more deeply into Your kingdom within me. I release any thoughts of sinfulness which would try to convince me that I am unworthy to be healed. I want to remove any blocks within me which would interfere with Your spirit so that the healing work can be done within me.

Loving Lord God, I cannot heal myself nor be healed by anxious prayer. However, I proclaim I will be healed by Your gentle spirit as I accept more and more Your power within me. I now use the authority which Jesus has given me to tell me mind and body to function in accord with Your will.

You are a God of peace and harmony. It is Your will that Your children be happy and whole. I now remind myself of this truth and know it will set me free.

Loving Lord God, I ask for the vision to see myself as you see me: whole, forgiven, free from fear and guilt. I let Your love minister to me and let go of any defenses I have set up against Your love. I invite You into every part of my being and see Your light shining in me now.

(Pause for a while and let the light of Christ begin to grow within you. The spark of Divine Life is within you. Visualize the glorified body of Jesus and let that light penetrate all areas of pain. Take your time.)

## Listening Prayer for Continuous Healing

My child, I give you this present moment as a gift, a new creation. I give you opportunities to forget the past, to reach out to others in love and experience my presence in a new and lasting way. Live each precious moment in My presence. Be attentive to My voice as I speak to you in every circumstance of this day. All I ask of you is your little willingness to listen and obey. I go wherever you go. You are never alone or separated from My presence. I love you because I know you. My love for you is your strength. You have nothing to fear.

My child, each moment I ask you to do My will, to choose again and undo the past. Accept My unconditional love for you this present moment. I invite you to see through My eyes and take on My mind and heart. I am the light in which you see. I am the source of peace which you carry into every situation.

My child, peace is wherever you go, because it is within you. Be confident and unafraid because My Spirit lives within you. You will be taught how to heal and be healed.

My child, choose gratefulness and generosity this very moment. As you have freely received gifts, so freely give them to others. Give love away so that it may increase within you. Let no selfish thoughts dominate your mind when they arise, quietly look at hem, and gently let them go. Do not choose them. They bring only guilt, fear, and anger. Listen only to My voice. I will teach you the truth that will set you free.

My child, I am present in every person you meet this day. Honor and respect all who pass your way today because there are no accidents in My plan for salvation. Your healing depends on recognizing me in all you meet so that all may be healed.

Since I have chosen not to condemn you, you are not to condemn yourself or anyone. All your thoughts are powerful. Think only loving thoughts, for they alone are true and are the same as Mine. I am a God of consolation, not desolation. I have come not to condemn the world, but to bring it healing and salvation. I now send you to do the same!

My child, admit that you have made mistakes, but know that everything is correctable. Change your mind about yourself, and see yourself forgiven and free. Be patient with yourself. Time used by the Holy Spirit brings healing and relief. Relax in My love and stop trying to earn your healing. You are "born again" each day. Choose resurrection in place of crucifixion. Be humble before Me, but powerful in Me. Turn toward Me and away from sickness and disease. These are not My will.

My child, let go of the past without condemnation. Walk into the future without fear. This present moment is the moment of release. I love you! Trust your Brother Jesus, He knows what you need to be healed, and he will never deny you. He will supply you with everything you need. All he needs is your participation by your willingness to forgive. Remember, All is well! All is well! Because all is well in Christ.

## Prayer in Time of Distress

Loving Lord God, your child is not at peace. I must have made a decision by myself without consulting Your Holy Spirit. I must have misunderstood myself and my function here on earth. Now I choose otherwise because I want the peace which is my rightful inheritance as Your precious child.

I give these unholy feelings to the Holy Spirit who alone can retranslate them for me and undo the consequences of my mistakes.

Loving Lord God, I am attacking myself and hiding behind a smoke screen which I have set up to protect myself from Your love. I now choose to change my mind and see the loveliness and the beauty within me so that I no longer need defenses from you.

Loving Lord God, You are patient with me. Help me to be patient with myself. Help me never to demand more of myself or others than we are able to give. Help me not to substitute my plan for salvation in place of your gentle plan.

Holy Spirit, I give you this distressful thought...(I mention the thought specifically). I ask you to judge it for me. Help me not to see it as a sign of sin and guilt, nor to use it for destruction. Teach me not to use it as an obstacle to peace, but help me to use it as an opportunity for forgiveness and a reminder of Your presence within me. I give You my willingness to see this problem differently, despite the way I feel Exchange this unholy feeling for Your holy instant, the one that both You and I would rather have. I not only choose it for myself, but for all who come my way. I know I cannot have it unless I share it.

Loving Lord God, I come to you now and seek the peace which You alone can give. I come in silence and in gratitude, in the quiet of my heart and in the deep recesses of my mind. I wait for You and listen for Your voice. I come to hear You in stillness and in love, knowing that You will answer me.

Loving Lord God, I let all my fantasies and prejudices go. I allow the Holy Spirit to lead the way. The Holy Spirit alone knows the way. The Holy Spirit will never keep from me what I need to know so that peace may return to me.

Loving Lord God, in Your mercy, You have willed that I be free from this distress. Help me to step aside and to watch Your Spirit make my difficulties disappear, I turn within so that stately calm and holy stillness where dwells the Living God. Your love surrounds me. I am safe in your arms. Amen!

## Listening Prayer in Time of Distress

My child, be still! Lay aside all thoughts of what you think about yourself. Lay down your thoughts of danger and of fear. Lay down the cruel sword of judgment you hold against your throat let me remove the thorns and nails with which you have tried to crucify yourself. Lay aside all grievances by which you try to hide your holiness.

Let go of all concepts you learned about the world and all the images you hold against yourself. Empty your mind of everything you think is true or false, good or evil let go of thoughts you judge as worthy or thoughts of which you are ashamed. Do not bring with you one thought the past has taught you. Come to me with totally empty hands and an open mind. Forget this world for just a moment. You need do nothing. You need not know the way! Simply be still and rest in my presence and my love.

My child, it is not up to you to choose the way to Salvation. All you can do is choose to let me show the way. I am the Way, the Truth and the Life. No one knows the way to Truth but me. Ask me the way, and I will show you. Do not make demands or point the way that you should go. This is my function, and in your heart I will blaze the pathway. The way to God is simply to take my hand and let me lead and guide you. I will show you the open door through which infinite love shines outward from its home within you.

> My child, say slowly to yourself.
> The Light of God surrounds me.
> The Love of God enfolds me.
> The Power of God protects me.
> The Presence of God envelopes me.
> Wherever I am, God is.

Come to me, you who are weary and find life burdensome, and I will refresh you. You have long delayed, but now accept my call Leave everything behind and hear my call of love. It calls to you from deep within yourself, a place within your heart where dwells the True-Self you have forgotten.

My child, you are confused because you have forgotten who you truly are and what you really want. Hear my voice assuring you that all is well because you have not separated yourself from me. I knew you before you were born. I loved you then, and I have not changed my mind. My love still surrounds you and is within you. I love you because I know you. You do not love yourself because you do not know your True Self or see yourself as I do.

My love will provide for you. You need not worry about particulars; because my love is practical. Don't be trapped by lies. Do not judge yourself or tear yourself down. You cannot judge yourself because you don't know the truth about yourself. Leave all judgment to me. Only my judgments are true, and I have judged you worthy of my love. Be of good cheer, for I have overcome the world. Be easy on yourself. It is my will that you enjoy yourself today.

My child, submit all your practical decisions to my Holy Spirit today. When you hear his voice, you will have peace. You never need doubt about what you are to say or how you are to say it. My Holy Spirit will direct you. Stand on my promises! Act on your conviction that I am with you. Trust me! Celebrate your oneness with me today! Is there anything too marvelous for me to do? Is my hand shortened by your mistakes? Is there anything beyond my power to correct? Be humble before me, but all-powerful in me.

My child, take my hand!! Walk with me! No words are necessary. I gaze on you with love. Simply return that gaze. Do not fear. You stand on holy ground. I myself will provide for you. Just be still and know that I Am. Amen!

# Chapter 6

The Miracle of Who You Are.

Attain Inner Peace through Contemplation and Meditation

Prayer: Teach us, O Loving Lord God, to learn how to master life lessons, that we may live a life of peace, happiness, love and authentic self-identity. It is in you we want to live and move and have our being. Amen.

Let us pray:
0 Loving Lord God, You are awesome! I am so blessed. You are calling me to be with you in friendship. Your love is drawing me to enter into a deeper experience of you. Thank you for inviting me to be in your Presence. You have searched my heart O Lord. You have seen how much I need you. How much I have longed for you but did not know where to find you. You were right here closer than the breath I breathe. You are my one true love. May I always be aware that you are with me now and will be forever and ever. Amen.

Years ago when Father Peter McCall and I founded the prayer center in New York City we named it The House of Peace, for we believed that all healing begins at the core of our being with inner peace.

We were dedicated to bringing the good news of God's healing love to anyone who came to us afflicted in body, mind, or spirit. Countless numbers of people would ask us to pray that they receive peace of mind.

We of course would intercede, praying and assuring them of the unconditional love of Jesus. Unless someone has experienced this personal love themselves firsthand they will tend to rely on the assurances of those who have. There comes a time in one's own spiritual life, however, when The Holy Spirit has guided this soul in attaining inner peace through the method of contemplative prayer and meditation.

In our experiences we found that most people who came to us for prayer had a devastating self-hatred. There are a myriad of root causes why this is so.

We belong to the human race and we have been subjected to all types of behavior from the first day of our existence, even before we were born while we were in our mother's womb.

"The Secret Life of the Unborn Child" by Thomas Verney Md., (Dell Publishing Co. 1981) gives us research done with a number of expectant parents. The book is based on two decades of medical research on the unborn child. This research reveals some startling facts, especially that an unborn baby is an active, feeling human being, extremely sensitive to the parents' feelings about him or her.

I firmly believe that the fears of many generations past can be passed on and on and propagated until someone in a particular generation realizes the need to be healed and seeks after it.

Generational healing has become a popular form of healing prayer since the book, "Healing the Family Tree", by Dr. Kenneth McAll, MD, (Sheldon Press, London) was published in 1982.

Doctor McAll was a psychiatrist who discovered that

he could go only so far in helping a patient till he met with generational issues that could only be healed through prayer, especially the Eucharist.

He realized that there was still a connection between patients alive today and family members who had died, even many generations before. It seemed that if some relatives passed over to the other side with unfinished business, the present generation could still be carrying these issues.

This belief has become even more prevalent in our day with regard to the healing of addictions. We are aware that many diseases are passed down genetically. Biologically, this can be proven.

Now we have come to understand that even behavioral patterns can be multi-generational. Much of the violence and prejudice in our society is generational. Our healing ministry eventually had to address the issue of generational healing.

Generational healing is the healing of the "family flaw." We carry in our mind and body our family history. We all come into this world a "mixed bag," that is, we come with both healthy and unhealthy characteristics and family traditions. Generational healing aims at preserving the good from our inheritance and rejecting what is harmful.

Much of generational healing has to do with our cultural inheritance. Cultures are systems of practices and beliefs that are helpful in giving identity and structure to the lives of many people, but a culture can also cause dysfunctions when accepted behaviors of the group encourage shame and addictions.

The disease of alcoholism for example can be handed down culturally. Patterns of drinking have become lifestyles, not only for families but also for nations. Biologists tell us that we can inherit certain strengths and weakness.

Certain dispositions toward heart disease, cancer and other physical symptoms can be explained genetically. However, we are finding out that these family traits need not be passed down when generational healing prayer is practiced.

Just as an individual can be healed, physically through prayer, so a family line can be purified from undesirable traits which the family presumed was an inevitable part of their family tradition.

A family's religious tradition is a powerful influence on health and wholeness. How we see ourselves is determined in a large degree on how we are taught to view God. Fear of God has been a traditional technique to control behavior, and many times religious fanaticism has produced prejudices and racial disorders which have seriously affected spiritual growth and development.

So much of our violence and wars can be traced back to generational roots which have become a family tradition even though the original cause has been forgotten. So much of national pride is religious prejudice and it has not always had salutary effects on people and communities.

We also know today that certain emotional pathologies can have family roots. We are discovering that types of depression can be found in the family tree. Certain types of behavior such as violence, child abuse and suicide can become a family tradition by the process known as identification. We tend to identify with powerful models in our family and unconsciously imitate such behavior.

Before we begin to pray to be free of any destructiveness which we may have inherited from our family line, we must first express gratitude for what we have received that is good. Many family traits we have received have made life pleasant for us. A considerable number of the good things we take for granted today are the result of hard work and dedication of our ancestors.

Most of our immigrant forbearers suffered much so that we could have a good life. We have personality traits inherited from our ancestors that are beneficial to us. There are also physical and spiritual gifts we have received.

For example in my family line, there are artists, intellectuals, musicians and love of the earth manifested in gardening skills. I've also observed a tenacious nature in much of the family. We express our gratitude and ask for freedom from negativity with prayers of thanksgiving. Generational healing is the way we on earth can help those who went before us and help ourselves at the same time.

Let us pray:
Loving Lord God, We pray in the Holy Name of Our Lord, Jesus Christ as we ask for the grace to receive a grateful heart and mind  We thank you for the gift of our ancestors and for the positive loving attitudes and gifts that have been passed on down to us through the family tree. We acknowledge our gratitude to them for the courage it took to persevere in the midst of hardships. Thank you for all the many physical, spiritual and creative gifts we have received.
(Here name some of the gifts you inherited from your family.)
Lord it is so easy for us to focus on the negative instead of seeing the beautiful and wondrous ways in which you have blessed us through the lives who came before us, Help us to continue to develop our minds to appreciate and to be grateful. We love you and praise your holy name now and forever. Amen.

Generational healing through prayer is based on the doctrine and belief of the Communion of Saints. What this doctrine really teaches is that we are all, living and deceased, connected in some way.

Generational healing is basically healing of relationships. We can not afford to hold grudges against anyone, even the deceased. Only in freeing others can we ourselves experience freedom.

We in the Catholic tradition believe in having Masses said for the deceased. The celebration of the Eucharist is a powerful prayer for generational healing.

As far as the living are concerned, all relatives who seem to be under generational bondage to the family "flaw" should be prayed for in a special way. All sicknesses and diseases which seem to be inherited must be rejected.

If you are able to have the good fortune of knowing a priest who would be open to celebrating a generation healing Mass, this would be ideal. At the Eucharist a family tree may be submitted at the offertory with all this information on it.

After this, we trust the prayer of Jesus to free and heal us. However if a priest is not available we can offer up prayers for our loved ones in our private observances.

The best form of prayer that we can do for both our living and deceased relatives is the prayer of forgiveness. Jesus told us all, *"Whatever you bind on earth shall be bound in heaven; whatever you loose on earth shall be loosed in heaven." (Mt. 18:18)* If we want to be free, we must be willing to free others through forgiveness.

Let us pray for forgiveness:
Loving Lord God, there is so much mystery concerning this subject of Generational healing. However we do know that Jesus Christ, Our Loving Savior, has surrendered his life for us so that we may live. His Resurrection from the dead has assured us of eternal life. We will put aside this familiar form and enter into another mysterious dimension of existence. We are but a thought away; still living but unseen.

Comforted by this knowledge we seek to be reconciled by the act of forgiveness to those loved ones in our family who have gone beyond, but left without completing their mission here on earth. (*Here place the names of those deceased family members, departed ancestors who may come to your mind.*)_____

_____

_____

_____

We thank you for the consoler, The Holy Spirit who comforts us in our grief. We grieve and mourn the losses and the regrets. We thank you also for the grace of forgiveness. We desire to move on to the path of living life fully until the time our mission here is accomplished. Then we will be able to join our loved ones in eternity.

Creator God, we offer you a prayer of praise and thanksgiving for having created us in your image and likeness. We have been formed to be heirs to the Kingdom of Heaven here on earth. We acknowledge and affirm that we cannot inherit from you O loving God, anything of this world that is evil. Nor can we inherit sickness, poverty, depression, or addictions, or any other dysfunction from you who are perfect love, and perfect goodness. We are your children, and we were created to inherit your essence. You are a God of the living therefore we cannot inherit death from you. We proclaim liberation from this world's limitations through our inheritance as children of the Most Wondrous and Magnificent High God. We thank you for our finest attributes of love, peace, joy and wisdom. We thank you for the opportunities you have presented to us to become peacemakers for ourselves, our loved ones both living and deceased and for future generations. Jesus has given each of us the power to forgive so we choose to forgive and ask to be forgiven. We let go of any harmful thoughts towards others and unleash anyone and everyone. We pray for those deceased that they may be emancipated from the bondage of remorse and

regrets. May they be granted the grace of forgiving themselves and also be aware that we in turn, forgive their offenses against us. We give them permission to be free as
we in turn, are freed.

Through the sacrificial act of love by Our Lord and Savior
Jesus Christ we are created anew and restored to our original state of union with God who is All.

All honor and glory and wisdom and love belong to our beloved God and Lord, Jesus Christ along with the Holy Spirit.
Thank you. Amen.

Dysfunctions in families are propagated by family secrets and denial. We can no longer afford to keep quiet
about the behaviors and sicknesses, mental and physical, of past members in the family system.

Our present generation and future generations need
a healthier consciousness and enlightenment so as to
bring about this awareness of the Divine in our lives.
Our true inheritance is from the Source of all life, that
which we call God. We are precious people, beloved of
God. This awareness of our true identity can be accomplished through the continued practice and discipline of
contemplative prayer.

### For the Wonder of Who I Am

The following exercise is a preparation for a meditation
based on Psalm 139, a beautiful psalm declaring the
All-knowing and Ever-present God. The purpose of the
meditation is to help us enter into an inner stillness and
in the silence affirm and discover for ourselves the wonder of physical and inner beauty.

The Scriptures tell us that we were made in the image and likeness of God and that we have divine attributes (Re: Gn. 1:26-27). But not too many people believe that God looks lovingly upon us and finds us to be

very good. If we are serious in our spiritual search and yearning for *"the peace that passes all understanding"* *(Philippians 4:7)* in time we will discover how precious we really are.

Throughout the meditation we will be using the affirmation *"For the wonder of who I am I thank you, Lord."* *(Re: on Psalm 139)*

One of the first steps we must learn in order to meditate and attain inner peace is to prepare for ourselves a period of time where we can relax. This means you need to find a time and place where you will feel comfortable and safe in a sitting position.

When you feel you are ready try breathing slowly. If you have taken any yoga courses or Lamaze training, then you will know how to do this. Begin by breathing slowly bringing the breath into the nose and extending the breath as far down to the lungs as you are capable of. Then slowly breathe out through the mouth.

Repeat this breathing process until you feel ready to do the meditation exercise. As you continue to breathe in, try to imagine you are breathing in sweetness and breathing out bitterness. Say it out loud to yourself.

"I breathe in sweetness and breathe out bitterness."

"I breathe in life and breathe out death wishes."

"I breathe in light and breathe out darkness."

"I breathe in joy and breathe out depression."

"I breathe in love and breathe out fear."


In quiet and in stillness try to be aware of God's Presence. God is ever-present. The God of Love is with you now and forever. Where can I go from your spirit? From your presence where can I flee?

If I go up to the heavens, you are there; if I sink to the nether world, you are present there.

If I take wings of the dawn, if I settle at the farthest

limits of the sea, even there your hand shall guide me and your right hand holds me fast. If I say *"Surely the darkness shall hide me, and night shall be my light. For you darkness is not dark, and night shines as the day."* *(Psalm 139:7-12)*

The Psalm is telling us we are always in God's loving Presence. Unless this has become a practice in our lives we will not know this, because the events of our daily lives keep us too occupied to notice.

In the spiritual life this is called the "veil of forgetfulness." There are just too many distractions in this world holding us unaware. In the New Testament, in the Gospel of Matthew, Jesus reminds us we are never alone. The Lord has promised to remain with us always even until the end of the world. (Re: Mt. 28:20)

Return to and continue to breathe in and out slowly. Quiet your mind. Say to *yourself "Be still and know that I am God." (Psalm 46:10)* Repeat this mantra until you feel the stillness. God's unconditional love is around you and in you, surrounding and enfolding you in a blanket of comfort and safety. This love is closer than the breath you breathe.

Meditate for a few moments, saying, "I am loved." "I am loveable." Affirm these statements over and over again. Give yourself permission to rest in this sweet, loving Presence. Allow yourself to surrender to this love, physically, emotionally, spiritually.

Take all the time you need. There can be no rushing this process. And you don't have to do it perfectly. This is not about perfection. This is about learning a whole new process of listening to that still inner voice.

Continue to be aware of your breath and breathe slowly. Eventually let go of any ideas and thoughts and say to yourself, "For the wonder of who I am, I thank you, Lord." Again, "For the wonder of who I am, I thank you, Lord." Allow the peace that only this Presence can bring to permeate your mind and spirit. Say to yourself, "I am in God's presence, God is all there is."

Reflect and permit these thoughts to have an effect on your body beginning with your feet, wiggling your toes and relaxing the toes, the arch of the foot and the ankles. Focus on peace in your mind and bring it to the calves of your legs, knees and under the knees and thighs, buttocks. Let go and relax...and breathe. Repeat to yourself, "I am peaceful." "I am loved."

Our body is wonderfully made. Allow your mind to focus on the lower back, bring peace to it and allow it to travel up through all the vertebrae and to the back of the neck.

Continue to remind yourself to relax and be at peace. Allow your shoulders to be relaxed, as your head is beginning to feel heavy now. You are in God's healing presence now. God is with you. Let your forehead, your eyes, your cheeks and mouth relax gently.

Peace enters your throat area and moves down slowly into your chest, heart, lungs, stomach, intestines, and internal organs, genitals, moving down to the thighs, legs, ankles, and toes.

Remind yourself once again... "I am in the presence of God's healing love." Remain calm and serene allowing this Divine Presence to do the work of healing. God's loving presence fills your mind. Rest in this presence, and in this loving experience.

You have prepared the way for a conscious awakening to the realization that there is only One Love and that is God. We cannot look to others for the love we need but rather allow God's love to flow to us and out to others.

So in doing this exercise you are opening yourself to being loved by the Source of all Love. Allow this love energy to infiltrate every cell of your entire being. Repeat again, "For the wonder of who I am I thank you Lord. For the miracle of my mind and body I thank you Lord."

The Divine Presence radiates a brilliant energy of shining light. This pure energy is a healing power being poured out from the throne of Grace.

Beginning at the crown of your head, see this light entering in at this point. Your body is composed of billions and billions of cells and atoms infused with this life-filled energy, this glorious, shining light.

See it flowing into your brain cells. Feel your brain cells being flooded with new life. This shining energy of light is activating the workings of your mind, the awareness of being enlightened by God's holy Presence. Your mind and Divine mind are as one holy and enlivened mind.

We only think we are separate from our Divine Creator but in fact we are never separated. Our thoughts create separation. Quietly say, "I am being transformed by the renewal of my mind. I am operating with a clear and sound mind. My life is ever changing and my mind is ever new. I am an intelligent being. With God's enlightening power, I make intelligent choices. For the miracle of my mind and intelligence, I thank you, Lord."

Focus your mind to the center of your forehead between the eyes. Say to yourself, "In God I live and move and have my being."

God's procreative energy produces new life and restores energy to areas of our body that tend to be depleted from giving out so much of ourselves to the world's activities. Allow this restorative power to fill you up. Breathe it in and partake of its strength saying quietly, "I am being restored and strengthened in every part of my body, mind and soul. For the wonder of who I am I thank you Lord."

Focus your attention on your eyes and say, "The radiance of God's love shines in my eyes. For the wonder of my eyes I thank you, Lord. My eyes see clearly with the light that shines forth from the Throne of God. God gazes lovingly upon me and I am in awe."

Bring your awareness to your ears, saying, "God's healing light enters my ears and all the inner workings of my ear. This light fills my hearing with sweet sounds. My ears hear with clarity. I listen with love to the goodness that surrounds me. For the miracle of my ears and hearing, I thank you, Lord."

With the light directed to the throat area, say, "I speak with the voice of truth and honesty. My voice is an instrument of healing words spoken with love as my motivation. I express myself freely, joyously, lovingly. I sing a song of love. I communicate words of encouragement and peace. I choose to use my voice for the sake of blessing. For the wonder of my voice, I thank you, Lord."

Bring your awareness to the nape of your neck and say, "I choose to be more adaptable and free; I choose to see all sides of the issue. It is safe to see another point of view."

"I choose peace instead of conflict. I am safe. For the wonder of who I am, I thank you, Lord."

Continue to relax and then release other people and their cares. Turn them over to the loving care of God. "Let go and let God." Love your family and friends but let the God of their understanding direct their lives.

As we gradually are set free from self-centeredness we are freed from the tendency to find fault, gossip, criticize, or take offense. As we become more God-centered we begin to be more understanding, gentle, and wise.

Turn your attention to your shoulders now. Release your shoulders from the burdens of the past, present, and future. Say, "By God's grace I am released. By grace I receive all the help I need in order to live a peaceful and healed life." "Help me to be aware of my need to trust in you more so that I will know you are taking care of me." Allow yourself to feel your burdens being lifted and dissolved in the healing light of God's love.

With your mind, gently move the healing light down along the spinal column. The light touches and fills each vertebra with energy and health. Slowly moving down the spine, the light eventually rests at the small of the lower back. Affirm to yourself, "I am being supported by a loving God. "God is my advocate."

"I am trusting God to take care of all of my needs. I am in God's loving care and I am safe."

"I need not be anxious or afraid for God is with me."

"For the wonder of who I am I thank you Lord."

Truly you have formed my inmost being. You knit me in my mother's womb. I give you thanks that I am fearfully and wonderfully made; wonderful are your works.

*"My soul also you knew full well, nor was my frame unknown to you when I was made in secret, when I was fashioned in the depths of the earth. Your eyes have seen my actions, in your book they are all written; my days were limited before one of them existed. How weighty are your designs, O God, how vast the sum of them! Were I to recount them, they would outnumber the sands: did I reach the end of them I should still be with you." (Psalm 139:13-18)*

*"Probe me, O God, and know my heart; try me and know my thoughts." (Psalm 139:23)*

Now imagine your heart bathed in Divine Light. Place your hand on your heart. Feel the pulsing beat of your heart under your hand. The heart is the seat of emotions. Realize the love of our Creator God desiring to heal any brokenness of heart.

Our Lord wants you to feel this warm, all embracing love. You are beloved of God and to experience this perfect love first-hand is a gift, releasing you from your fears. *"Perfect love casts out all fear" (1 Jn. 4:18)* As you place your hand on your heart affirm for yourself, "Perfect love casts out all fear."

If you have devotion to the Sacred Heart of Jesus, it is helpful to imagine his heart burning with love for you. I often ask Jesus to unite my broken heart with His Heart burning with love for me. The pure love of Christ purifies and heals the pain that I am feeling at the time.

All healing involves forgiveness on some level. With God's unconditional love in mind, try to remember if there is anyone in this present moment you need to forgive. Take your time with this. When someone or a situation comes to your mind, simply allow the love of God to free them and you from the past event.

"Let Go and let God." Give them permission to go in peace. Do not be concerned whether they are living or dead. All you need do is to ask for the grace of willingness to forgive.

Our loving God knows how to heal our wounded hearts. Affirm for yourself: "My heart releases the wounds of the past, and I am forgiven. I am beloved of God. My heart beats harmoniously to the rhythm of God's love. Love is all there is. God's love fills and sustains me. My heart is holy ground, for God's love dwells there. I am loved and loveable, I am one with God and God is one with me. For the miracle of my heart, I thank you, Lord."

The circulatory system carries the blood to all the parts of the body and internal organs. Bless the intricacy of the blood vessels, the veins and arteries carrying the blood that flows harmoniously throughout the circulatory system.

Say to yourself, "I am regenerating and circulating new life within me. Peace is flowing through my veins and arteries. The joy of living is circulating freely within me. Divine light is flowing through me and out to all I encounter. My life belongs to God. For the wonder of your works, I thank you, Lord."

Extend this radiant divine light into the lungs and

respiratory system. Breathe in deeply the glorious breath of Life, God's Life. Breathe out stifling thoughts and fears that rob you of life. Breathe in healing energy. Breathe out thoughts of death and dying. Breathe in healing light.

Say, "God created me for a specific reason and I have a right to be here." Breathe in the aroma of health. Fill the lungs and respiratory system with wholesome fresh air. Breathe in deeply the gift of being alive. Ask and receive zeal for newness of life. I am welcomed and received with love and approval."

"God saw all that was created and declared it good. I am God's wonderful miracle of creation. I choose to live life in all its fullness and abundance. I am excited about life. I send peace and serenity into my lungs. All is well, I am loved. For the wonder of my life, I thank you, Lord."

Focus your mind on the light within and focus the light on the digestive tract beginning with the esophagus. Bring the healing light to the stomach area, the large and small intestines, affirming as you do so, "I am digesting the life God has given me more easily. I am absorbing and assimilating new experiences with peace and joy. I am trusting in the enfoldment of my life for God is with me, leading and guiding me. Only God's love can satisfy my hunger and my thirst. I am sustained by the awareness of being infinitely loved. As I rest in God's love, I am satisfied. For the wonder of who I am I thank you Lord."

Sending the healing light towards the elimination system, saying, "I am releasing all that I no longer need in my life. I am releasing the past with God's love and forgiveness. I am letting go of debilitating fears. I am being freed of all the garbage in my life.

God's cleansing, purifying grace is removing the hurts, the angers, the guilt and the anxieties that want to cling to me. I am being cleansed by the holiness and sacredness of Divine Love. I expel shameful memories. Freedom from shame has been granted me and I am free indeed. I proclaim with gratitude... the wonder of your cleansing and purifying grace, I thank you, Lord."

We are sexual beings. Let us give thanks to Almighty God for the gift of our sexuality. We have bodies, but we are not just our body. Our sexuality embraces every aspect of our being, spiritual, emotional, and physical.

Accept your sexuality as part of who you are. Affirm by saying, "I acknowledge and respect who I am. My sexuality is part of who I am. My sexuality is good and wholesome. Every part of my body is wonderful. I hold myself in high esteem, I respect my body. My body is a temple of the Holy Spirit.

"I ask a blessing from the Divine Presence to make me aware of how precious a gift I am to this world. I ask to be healed of shame and guilt. Let it be replaced with appreciation and acceptance of my divine right as a beautiful person blessed by God. For the wonder of who I am, I thank you, Lord."

The grandeur of the central nervous system is a wonder to behold! God has given us an amazing network of organs and tissues that controls and coordinates all the activities of the body.

Its complexity and magnificence is astounding when we consider how our nervous system serves us to communicate messages and impulses to all parts of the body. Affirm by saying, "I communicate harmony, order, peace and tranquility to my central nervous system. I am a receiver of divine energy. My nervous system is receiving healthy messages of divine life and energy. I rest my nervous system in stillness and quiet and am renewed. For the miracle of who I am, I thank you, Lord."

Continue to affirm: "I am on a wonderful journey of self-discovery. My Lord helps me to be all that I can be and is helping me to reach my highest potential. In all my ways God helps me to maintain a healthy balance so that I can lead a more harmonious way of living life."

Your life is a gift. It is up to you whether you will accept that or not. You are a gift to this world.

*As we discover this light within and without, we will realize that the Holy Spirit is working out our life for us. Eventually we will relax in this wondrous love and become witnesses to the wonderful life God has given us. "For the wonder of your Love, I thank you Lord." (Re: Psalm 139)*

Let us pray:
Loving Lord God; I thank you for the gift of creation. I thank you for the gift of my life. You created me and had me in your mind from all eternity. Help me to see my life as a gift. Help me to be a light to the world this day. Show me the way to maintain my equilibrium as I learn to become the Love God created me to be. Show me the way to salvation this day and every day of my life. I turn my life and my will over to you, Wondrous God of Unconditional love and overflowing joy. Loving Lord God I need all the wisdom, intelligence, love and joy you have to give me in order to live life to the fullest. Without you I am nothing. I need you each and every moment of my existence. Help me to be all you want me to be. Your grace is sufficient to supply my every need. I thank you and Praise you now and forever. All Glory and honor belongs to you. Amen.

## Prayer for Generational Healing

Loving Lord God, Creator of us all we come before you knowing so much of life is mystery. Jesus has assured us that through His resurrection, we will live forever... We are grateful to you for sending Jesus Christ, Our Savior to our earth plane to show us how to live life to the fullest.

We will put aside this familiar form of life and enter into another dimension of existence. We are but a thought away; still living but unseen. We are comforted by this awareness and we seek to be reconciled through the act of forgiveness to those loved ones in our family who gone beyond, but left without finishing their mission. We who loved them need to grieve and mourn our losses. We desire to release them to you. We surrender them and let them go to be loved and healed. (*Mention the names of your loved ones*)_____

_____

_____

Let us pray:

Loving God, help us to live life to the fullest and with you guiding us we will be able to fulfill our mission here on earth. God of love, God of wisdom, Jesus has admonished us in Holy Scripture to call no one on earth our Father. We have been instructed that you are our Heavenly Father. You are also Spirit and Perfect Pure Essence. You are our Creator. We have been born here to fulfill a destiny. We have been created to love and be loved. Since you are our True and Real Parent, we acknowledge we cannot inherit any evil from you. We do not inherit sickness, poverty, depression or addictions from you. We do not inherit death from you since you are a God of the Living. We proclaim liberation from the world's limitations through our inheritance as Children of the Most High, Most Magnificent and Glorious God of Pure Love. We can only inherit goodness, joy, peace, compassion, gentleness, loving kindness, wisdom, knowledge, and pure, and, holy love, eternal love.

O Lord, we thank you for all the opportunities you have given us to continue to forgive and to release our loved ones both living and departed We include all future generations since there is no time or space in your Kingdom of Love. Thank you for the gift of our free will, the gift to choose to be peacemakers for ourselves and for our loved ones. Jesus has instructed us to forgive and to forgive again. We choose to forgive those of our ancestry who may have passed their errors down to us. We release and unleash anyone and everyone. We choose to forgive ourselves for mistakes we made. We pray for those departed ones so that they may be emancipated from the bondage of regrets and remorse. We pray for those who were unable to accomplish their purpose here on earth. We pray for those who have passed on their pain to us. We pray they be granted the grace to forgive themselves. We also pray that we may forgive them for their offenses against us. We choose to give and receive peace to those in this world and in the beyond. We thank you for the freedom of soul you have given us, 0 most wondrous and loving God  Through the redeeming and healing love of Our Lord , Jesus Christ  we continue our journey in returning to our original state of union with God . We proclaim God who is Perfect Love, God who is perfect joy, God who is Perfect Peace, God who is Perfect Wisdom. We are victorious for we are victorious in Christ. Blessed be the Lord of Love and Life. Amen and Amen!

*"In Him we live and move and have our being." (Acts 17:28)*

Pictures

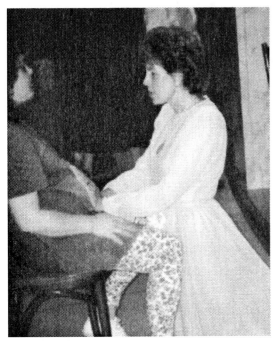

Maryanne praying
with mother and
unborn child at the
House of Peace.

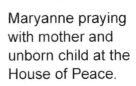

*Lower right:*
Father Peter McCall
and Maryanne Lacy
with a portrait of the
Venerable Solanus
Casey (1870-1957),
miraculous healer and
intercessor for the
Healing Ministry.

*Lower left:*
Oral Roberts invited Maryanne and
Father Peter for a visit to the City of
Faith, Tulsa, Oklahoma, where they
had private prayer time in his office.

Father Peter was a fan of Rosemary Clooney and Julius LaRosa. They surprised him by inviting us to a club in Manhattan where she was performing. Rory LaRosa, Julius's wife was a volunteer at the House of Peace during the early years.

Dr. and Mrs. Bernie Siegel gave a talk for the House of Peace on "The Exceptional Cancer Patient" to a sell-out audience one year prior to his ground breaking best seller, *Love, Medicine and Miracles.*

Blessed Sacrament Monastery Chapel in Yonkers, NY, was the setting for the Healing Masses held on first Saturday of each month until the Sisters sold the property in the late 1980s.

The House of Peace relocated to a facility owned by the Faustini/Mariani family in the Bronx, NY.

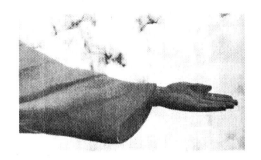

# Chapter 7

Healing: a Call to Holiness

Giving and Receiving the Gifts of God

Prayer: O loving Lord God, you have called us in love to be pure and holy in your sight. We pray and ask for the grace we need in order to be a loving channel of your peace, joy and goodness. Teach us O Divine and holy One to be lovers of your guidance and inspirations. Grant us the grace of holy intuition so that we may be attuned to your will as you lead us on in this journey of sacred discovery. We adore you O most wondrous and loving lord. We praise the glorious name of Jesus Christ, the Son of the Living God. All glory and honor belong to you now and always. Amen.

*"Praise be the God and Father of Our Lord Jesus Christ who has bestowed on us in Christ every spiritual blessing in the heavens! God chose us in him before the world began to be holy and blameless in his sight, to be full of love." (Eph. 1:3-4).*

Both Father Peter McCall and I were drawn to the healing ministry because we were in need of healing ourselves. We had experienced the healing power of Jesus and so were compelled to share this power with others. We learned rather quickly that all we can do in the healing ministry is to introduce people to the real healer–Our Lord and Savior Jesus the Christ.

We were convinced that once people knew Jesus as he truly is–Savior, Redeemer and Healer, that people would flock to him as they did when he was on earth in his physical form. And they do. There can be no turning back once we have experienced this extraordinary love.

The desire for holiness or unity with God has to be the chief reason we pursue this spiritual journey. In reality I believe it is God who is pursuing us; wooing us back to our truth. *"A highway will be there, called the holy way..." (Is. 35:8)*

When I longed for peace in my life, I never gave a thought to becoming a holy person, it was the furthest thing from my mind. I was too wounded, too broken in spirit to even consider what that meant. In the midst of all that hurt and pain, Jesus knew my heart and the deepest desires of my soul. He knew before I did, that the love I needed and sought was in him and him alone.

It was He who broke through all the barriers and defenses I had placed up to protect myself. It was Jesus who drew me to his bosom by his incredibly powerful gift of love. St. Paul writes, *"God chose us in him before the world began, to be holy and blameless in his sight."* *(Eph. I:4)*

Isn't it just amazing that the Lord of the Universe chose you and me to become holy and guilt free even before the world began? It is far beyond my frail human imagination.

Thank you Lord for choosing us to be holy vessels of your sweet, sweet love. Blessed be the Holy One, the Lord God of heaven and earth. Amen.

Paul prays, *"May the God of peace make you perfect in holiness. May he preserve you whole and entire, spirit, soul (psyche) and body, irreproachable at the coming of our Lord, Jesus Christ. He who calls us is trustworthy, therefore he will do it." (1 Thes. 5:23-24)*

After the experience of the Baptism of the Holy Spirit I described in Chapter One, I did begin to feel that I was aware of being in God's loving presence. I gradually began to grow in the knowledge of what can only be described as a desire for more of who I was in the light of this new found experience. Most of all I felt lavishly loved by God.

The holiness of God's love overwhelmed and touched every aspect of who I was. Everything else in my life seemed so mundane and senseless. I felt an enormous release from inner turmoil and a humble gratitude for the peaceful awakening my soul was experiencing. I felt loved beyond the ordinary for a good long while and I am sure some people I knew thought I was on some mood altering drug. Nonetheless it was the beginning of a fascinating relationship with the God I have come to know as pure and perfect unconditional love, overflowing joy and Wisdom of the Universe.

It also was the beginning of many spiritual and temporal lessons I had to learn in order to grow. At this point I was as a nursery school child in the Kingdom of God. It was necessary to allow The Holy Spirit to teach me how to remove the blocks to the unhealed unconscious part of me in order to grow in holiness.

Eventually I had to let go of negative beliefs and faulty attitudes about God, myself, others and the world around me. I had to be purified from the belief that I was separated from God. This is a lesson I am still in the process of learning. *"You must put on that new person created in God's image whose justice and holiness are born of truth." (Eph. 4:24)*

A slogan that we have used very often in our work is, "Healing is not so much what we do– as what we undo."

Let us pray:

0 Great loving and eternal God, I come before you as a little child in simplicity. I am in the process of seeking love and the way to holiness. I desire to be set free from anything that would sway me from this path. I believe in your love for me and I trust you to provide me with the tools I need in order to remove the obstacles from the course I have chosen to be with you. I pray you would heal me of my sense of unworthiness. I have felt I had no right to be worthy of your love. I ask to be healed from a false sense of humility. I do want to be humble 0 Lord, but in the true sense of the word. I want to be set free from any self-deception that would lead me to believe I am unworthy to become holy. Help me to believe in myself as a child of God. Touch my mind and my spirit with the truth of your holy word. I thank you 0 Lord for listening to my plea. I believe you are listening and always hear my prayer. I love and adore you now and forever. Blessed be your holy essence. I pray this in the holy name of our Lord and Savior Jesus Christ. Let it be done by the power of the Holy Spirit. Amen.

## Blocks to Growing in Holiness

The most prominent blocks to the awareness of our growing in holiness is in the area of self-deception. These are deceptions we have relied on that keep us from believing in our true identity. One of these deceptions revolves around our self-image and this might include a devastating inferiority complex in which our sense of self is so poor that we find it hard to believe that God could love us.

We were often told in the past that pride is the root of all evil. We have found in praying with people through the years that self-hatred and self-condemnation are far more damaging to the life of the soul. In fact if we really understood that we are God's holy creation, we would be proud of our identity. Paul says, *"Let him, who would boast, boast in the Lord." (I Cor. 1:31)*

Once we accept and believe that we are precious in the eyes of God we can boast that we are God's children. When we give glory to God for revealing to us our true identity we give honor to our Creator. We don't do homage to God when we demean ourselves. We glorify God by acknowledging the good we have received and believing in our own innate goodness. Paul writes, *"Everything God created is good; nothing is to be rejected when it is received with thanksgiving; for it is made holy by God's word and by prayer." (1 Tm. 4:4)*

Let us pray:
0 loving and eternal God we offer our gratitude to you for revealing your love to us. We praise and thank you that you have declared us holy and precious in your sight. Open our eyes so we may see ourselves as you see us. Grant us the grace we need in order to fully accept ourselves as children of the most high and gracious God. Continue to free us from self-deception. Heal us of the root cause of our poor self-image. We desire to become the holy people you have created us to be. Grant us all we need in the becoming of our highest state of goodness and holiness. We thank you, 0 most loving and merciful Savior. God, you are so good. Alleluia. Amen.

Father Peter taught that the most deceptive lie introduced into western spirituality was the distortion of the doctrine of grace known as "merit." The whole concept of merit is a contradiction of Paul's letter to the Romans which clearly states... "Everything is grace." (Rom. 4:13)

In other words, everything is a gift from God who loves perfectly. Our function is not to earn our holiness or healing, but to accept it as a free gift from a benevolent God. So many people plead with God in their prayers hoping to overcome God's resistance to their need. Scrupulosity in the religious life is a sense of a gnawing uneasiness or anxiety with deep rooted feelings of guilt. People who suffer from scrupulosity feel they have to please God at any cost mostly through countless religious practices or mortifications. The motivation behind this is to placate and appease a harsh perception of God.

We knew a gentleman who was an agoraphobic– that is an abnormal fear of being outside the safe environment of a home base. Whenever Father Peter was free to do so he would visit this gentleman and hear his confession. Eventually this gentleman decided to call him at the office of the House of Peace every day to confess his daily sins.

No matter how often Father Peter would try to convince him that God has surely forgiven him it never eased his fears for very long. He would be fine while Father Peter listened and gave him absolution but the next day he was filled with the scruples of a guilty conscience.

In our many years of doing healing services, we would inevitably be aware of some people in the congregation who would be weighed down with numerous holy items around their neck such as medals, scapulars, rosaries and crosses– used for protection against some deep rooted, unknown fears. We knew people who said rosary after rosary and novena after novena. There is nothing wrong with wearing a holy medal or saying the rosary or doing a novena.

When it is done disproportionately and in excess to appease and break down God's resistance to their pleadings it becomes a big obstacle to a soul's growth in holiness. Scrupulosity is a fearful sickness of soul that needs the healing love of a gentle and kind Savior.

When we realize that everything is a gift from God

we can follow Paul's advice, *"Dismiss all anxieties from your minds. Present your needs to God in every form of prayer and in petitions full of gratitude. Then God's own peace, which is beyond understanding, will stand guard over your hearts and minds in Christ Jesus"* (Phil. 4:6-7).

Another deplorable deception that would block our awareness of God's love and to our own personal holiness would be how God is viewed as a hard taskmaster by many people. Too much evil in the world is justified as sent by God. This deception sees suffering and pain as something sent by God.

This faulty view of God would see cancer, AIDS and other diseases and disasters as God's way of dealing with his people and the world.

We came to believe and understand... *There is nothing but love in God.* We made this statement as a slogan for our work and printed it up on as many items as we could. We had a banner displayed at our healing services with the words, "There is Nothing but Love in God" written in bold letters and colors.

The truth is that the will of God for us always means greater freedom and a more abundant and grace filled life. We will never seek holiness, union with God, if we think God is the author of pain and suffering and destruction. We would want to avoid such a union as we would with any person we perceive as capable of violence.

The opposite of love is not hatred, but fear. *"Love has no room for fear; rather, perfect love casts out all fear. And since fear has to do with punishment, love is not perfect in one who is afraid. We, for our part, love because He loved us first."* (1 Jn. 4:18-19)

Once our unhealthy fear of God is healed, there are no more obstacles to holiness. Although the Scriptures speak of, *"...fear of the Lord, the true reference behind this statement is that God's Love is so far above our thoughts*

*that all we can do is bow down in reverence and awe."*
*(Heb. 12:28)*

> Let us pray:
> O most wondrous and loving Lord God, we come before you in deep humility realizing that we are the created and you are the Creator. Our souls yearn to know you as you truly are without fear and without doubt. Grant us the grace we need to rise up above the limited and negative images of you that have been fed us in the past. You are calling us to a new vision, a truer understanding of your Divine and holy nature. Illuminate us with the truth. Awaken within us a sense of your utmost glory and light.
> Loving Lord Jesus, we desire to behold your burning furnace of love for all humankind and for us personally and we long to be caught up in your transcendence. We long to participate in your Reality. It is with awe and reverence of your divine splendor that we come before you now and we choose to understand you as you truly are; A God of overflowing joy and absolute clarity and all that is totally good. We lift our hearts and minds in gratitude to you for revealing to us your Radiant and dazzling Light. We worship you O Lord, now and forever. Amen.

Another obstacle to true holiness would be a Pharisaic mentality...that is practicing or advocating a strict observance of external forms and ceremonies of religion or conduct without regard to the spirit. It would include sanctimonious and self righteous attitudes.

We find examples in the New Testament Gospels where Jesus would have confrontations with the Pharisees regarding the excesses of religious practices and ignoring the principle of love to one's neighbor. Jesus instructs us, *"I tell you, unless your holiness surpasses that of the scribes and Pharisees you shall not enter the* kingdom of God." (Mt. 5:20)

He goes on to say, *"The scribes and the Pharisees have succeeded Moses as teachers, therefore, do everything they tell you. But do not follow their examples. Their words are bold but their deeds are few. They bind up heavy loads, hard to carry, to lay on other men's shoulders, while they themselves will not lift a finger to budge them. All their works are performed to be seen. They widen their phylacteries and wear huge tassels. They are fond of places of honor at banquets and the front seats in synagogues, of marks of respect in public, of being call Rabbi."* (Mt. 23:2-7)

In the Gospel of Luke Jesus confronts them again, *"Woe to you Pharisees! You pay tithes on mint and rue and all the garden plants, while neglecting justice and the love of God. These are the things you should practice, without omitting the others."* (Lk. 11:42)

Someone told me a story of going to the Blessed Mother's shrine in Lourdes, France. A woman was kneeling devoutly, apparently saying her rosary, when a tourist quite by accident brushed up against her. This woman angrily berated the tourist and swung her pocketbook at her much to the chagrin of everyone around.

Father Peter and I were invited by a prayer group to perform a healing service at a church in New York. After the teaching, we would usually begin to pray with people from the altar. I was praying with someone when the Pastor of the church came up and told me I could not pray on the altar in front of the tabernacle. Of course I moved away from that area.

We were in the habit of praying with everyone who came to the healing service until the line of people ended. This same Pastor began turning off the lights to let us know he wanted us to leave before we were finished praying with everyone.

Whenever instances like this arose, Father Peter

would take a breath and simply say to me, "Maryanne, these are just opportunities for forgiveness. We had to put up with too many Pharisees during the twenty plus years we worked together in the church. Forgiveness had to become a way of life for us and was a chastening gift in helping to remove obstacles towards holiness. As we work toward freeing ourselves with the help of the Holy Spirit from unhealthy attitudes and beliefs, we can then choose to enjoy practicing the Presence of God.

An obstacle to attaining the call to holiness is attachment. Attachment is the belief that something outside of God can give us pleasure. When our treasure is anything but God, we are always afraid it will be lost or stolen. Jesus says, *"Do not lay up for yourselves an earthly treasure. Moths and rust corrode; thieves break in and steal. Make it your practice instead to store up heavenly treasure, which neither moths nor rust corrode nor thieves break in and steal. Remember where your treasure is, there your heart is also...no one can serve two masters...seek first His Kingship over you, His way of holiness, and all these things will be given you besides."* (Mt. 6:19-34)

No one can ideally identify what true holiness means for us as individuals. We can read the Scriptures, and look to spiritual writers and mystics as guides. We can listen to mature, devout and godly theologians, but who can really say what holiness means for you or for me?

What may be a way of holiness for one may not be for another. How we attain holiness is in the relationship of an individual with the God of his/her understanding. One thing is certain; if we do seek holiness then we can never seek anything directly, but God alone. Everything else must be released. The conflict of serving two masters would be too much.

Goodness results from experiencing the love Jesus has for us. Once we know that we are loved, goodness becomes an expression of a relationship with the one, true Lover of our souls. We are good because God is good. The good things we do are in imitation of the God we worship. We do what God would do in a particular situation. What would God do? Hear what Jesus has to say; *"I solemnly assure you, the Son cannot do anything by himself he can only do what he sees the Father doing. For whatever the Father does, the Son does likewise. For the Father loves the Son and everything the Father does he shows him."* (Jn. 5:19)

It is the experience of God's love that most people desire and is a real need of all people. Praying for and with others is a sacred calling for all Christians. By practicing the presence of God we become a support system for a hurting world.

We must spend time in prayer because holiness is being in union with God. In the spiritual life it is called the "Unitive Way." Prayer carries us toward an awareness of our own transcendence. This may come about during a season of worship and thanksgiving rising from deep within ourselves, or it may be a matter of simply resting in the Lord's sweet presence.

Prayer leads us to a renewal in body, mind and spirit, helps us to be at peace within ourselves and the world around us. Prayer is essential in helping to strengthen our relationship with God, and encouraging us to draw closer to an ever deepening awareness of our own holiness. Prayer; in particular listening prayer, is the highest blessing we can give ourselves and others. It is my belief that God wants us to be our true selves, to reach our highest potential. Prayer is the blessed vehicle moving us towards inner peace and thus the kingdom of God within.

Holiness then is being in such a state of union with The Holy Spirit that we are able to discern when we are being given instructions. We are given divine guidance, and shown what we are to say and do and, where we are to go and, how we are to be. We are all called to becoming holy.

We are becoming holy without even realizing it when we are faithful to our life's calling from God. In that becoming we need to express our gratitude to The Holy Spirit our teacher, helper and advocate. Jesus tells us *"No one is good but God alone." (Mk. 10:18)* The Source of all goodness desires that we be an expression of the Divine life that dwells within us.

So we say:

Holy, holy, holy is the Lord God of Hosts! All holiness and glory and honor and adoration belongs to our beloved God. May the holy name of Jesus be exalted now and forever more. Alleluia! Amen.

*"To you, who have been sanctified in Christ Jesus, called to be holy, with all those everywhere who call upon the name of Our Lord Jesus Christ...their Lord and ours..." (1 Cor. 1:2)*

Prayer to Jesus:
Beloved of my heart and soul I walk towards you in loving gratitude. You are heaven's reflection and I yearn to bow down in humble adoration before your holiness. Help me dear beloved Jesus to be freed from the obstacles to peace within my mind. I yearn to know you and the unconditional love of our merciful God. Help me to see through your eyes, the eyes of forgiveness and understanding. Grant to me your shining grace that I may look upon your holiness, and thus see my own in your loving gaze. I yearn to have holy sight and see all that is true and beautiful. I yearn to see the light of heaven shining in holy thoughts. I glory in the day when I fully realize that I am God's holy creation. Your loving kindness has brought many miracles in my life. I never knew true happiness until your love touched me and transformed me.

You are the Light of the world. You are my true love and I believe I am also your true love as I carry the Christ light within me. Your perfect love drives out all fear and I behold your magnificent sweetness. Let all who have eyes to see and all who have ears to hear... God alone is perfect goodness and flawless holiness. Jesus the Christ is the holy begotten son of our perfect and loving God. He is our prince of peace, our soul's salvation, our one true love, our way to heaven.

O most loving and eternal God I long to gaze upon your lovely purity and holiness for in that holy sight I will see the reflection of heaven's love. I thank you for the holiness growing ever deeper within me. With your many graces I am transcending the limitations of this world for the unlimited love and overflowing joy of the Kingdom of God. I thank you for choosing me to help light up the world with Christ's vision of a healed creation. May God's handiwork behold the glory of all that is graced and blessed by our wondrous Lord and Savior Jesus the Christ. Amen and Amen. Alleluia.

Glory to God in the Highest and peace to all people on earth.

## The Holiness of Jesus

The Scriptures clearly tell us of the attractive power of Jesus and how huge crowds would gather wherever he made an appearance. (Re: Mt. 15:30) They not only marveled at his words, *"No man has spoken like this before,"* (Jn. 7:46) but they also marveled at his works, *"He has done all things well. He makes the deaf to hear and the mute to speak."* (Mk. 7:37)

Jesus drew people to himself because he was good. The healing ministry in the Church today is just an extension of the goodness of Jesus. Jesus healed the sick, not to draw attention to himself, but because of His and God's compassionate love.

Often people who have manifested the gift of healing are put on a pedestal when it is Jesus who should be lifted up and glorified. There is proneness in human nature to magnify the person with the gift rather than God, the giver of all gifts and who brings about the healing.

Healing authenticates God's love, not a person's sanctity. *"God is love; and he that dwells in love dwells in God and God in him." (1 Jn 4:16)*

Jesus is that perfect love, that perfect holiness, dwelling in us when we surrender to that love, and that is what makes us holy. Jesus healed the sick simply because he wanted them to experience the Kingdom of God in the here and now! Jesus drew people to himself so as to draw them into the knowledge of God's infinite love.

He revealed the true nature of God as healer, as One who gently corrects the mistakes we have made, especially the mistake that anything but love can come from God. Jesus was both teacher and healer and his mission on earth...even after his passion and death...was to show that, what people intend for evil, God can turn into good, (Re: Gen. 50:20) or, as Saint Paul said, *"All things work for good for those who love God," (Rom. 8:28)* or, *"Nothing can separate us from the love of God in Christ Jesus Our Lord." (Rom 8:39)*

Jesus came to teach and demonstrate the truth that everything in this life can help us and lead us to God. *"Everything is possible for the one who believes." (Mk 9:23)*

Jesus taught through miracles. Miracles happen as a result of prayer. Jesus spent many hours in prayer; *"... then he went out to the mountain to pray, spending the night in communion with God." (Lk. 6:12)*

Healing then is a call to holiness. The healing ministry of Jesus demonstrates that suffering is not from God. If it was from God, why then did Jesus heal? Wouldn't he have been violating God's will that people should suffer in order to enter the Kingdom? By healing people Jesus knew it was God's will that they be freed from suffering. The only suffering Jesus promised his followers was persecution.

*"Peter was moved to say to him, 'We have put aside everything to follow you.' Jesus answered: 'I give you my word, there is no one who has given up home, brothers or sisters, mother or father, children or property, for me and for the gospel who will not receive in this present age a hundred times as many homes, brothers and sisters, mothers, children and property -and persecution besides- and in the age to come, everlasting life.'"* (Mk. 10:28-30)

Persecution is suffering imposed from external circumstances. This is the kind of suffering that Jesus himself experienced in his passion and death.

The suffering we experience from just being human that is associated with stress, anxiety, fear, and guilt are internal. There is no record that Jesus endured this sort of suffering. As far as we can tell from scripture, Jesus was a strong and healthy person. I imagine him in my mind traveling long distances along dusty roads in sandals, climbing hills and walking from village to village. Having been to the Holy Land three times I can testify to the rocky hills and roads.

There also is no record that Jesus believed sickness was sent by God. If sickness came from God, Jesus would not have healed it. The holiness of Jesus drew people to God by showing them that all the bad things they believed about God were just not true. God's solution to our sicknesses and this kind of suffering is to reveal the love that Jesus exhibited through his miraculous healing power.

I believe God wants to make us whole in body, mind and spirit. This means we need to have a healthy understanding of our body as well as developing healthy attitudes and concepts of ourselves and God. *"You must know that your body is a temple of the Holy Spirit, who is within-the Spirit you have received from God."* (1Cor. 6:19)

Jesus Christ did many miraculous works in the time he spent on earth. His mission was to establish a kingdom of love, peace and justice. The kingdom of God is among us and working in the ordinary situations of daily life. We are given many opportunities to experience this kingdom because God is living within us in each present moment.

When we experience hardships we can go within to where God dwells and ask for help and the solution will come if we listen. Jesus remains with us through the power of his resurrection and has sent us an advocate, the Holy Spirit so that we would be able to continue the work he began more than 2000 years ago.

*"Anything you ask me in my name I will do, if you love me and obey the commands I give you, I will ask the Father and he will give you another Paraclete to be with you always: The Spirit of truth." (Jn. 14:14-17)*

The Holy Spirit is the presence of Jesus here on earth. The Holy Spirit provides us with gifts, graces and fruits so that we will not be lacking in any good thing.

Jesus Christ came to this earthly plane in order to teach us the truth by revealing to us a God of total mercy, kindness and love. In Jesus we have the fullness of life, *"It pleased God to make absolute fullness reside in him" (Col. 1:19)* and *"I came that they may have life, and have it abundantly." (Jn. 10:10)* and *"He has put all things under Christ's feet and has made him, thus exalted, head of the church, which is his body; the fullness of him who fills the universe in all its parts." (Eph. 1:22-23)*

When Jesus Christ lived here on earth He proclaimed the good news of the Kingdom by healing the sick. When John the Baptist sent two of his disciples to ask Jesus if he really was the Christ or if they should look for another, he said, as proof that he really was sent from God: *"Go and tell John what you hear and see: the blind receive their sight and the lame walk, lepers are cleansed*

*and the deaf hear, and the dead are raised up, and the
poor have good news preached to them" (Mt. 11:4-5)*

*"Jesus left that place and passed along the Sea of
Galilee. He went up onto the mountainside and sat down
there. Large crowds of people came to him bringing with
them cripples, the deformed, the blind, the mute, and
many others besides. They laid them at his feet and he
cured them. The result was great astonishment in the
crowds as they beheld the mute speaking, the deformed
made sound, cripples walking about, and the blind seeing. They glorified the God of Israel." (Mt. 15:29-31)*

*"After making the crossing they came ashore at Gen-
nesaret, and tied up there. As they were leaving the boat,
people immediately recognized him. The crowds scurried
about the adjacent area and began to bring in the sick on
bedrolls to the place where they heard he was. Wherever
he put in an appearance, in villages, towns, or at crossroads, they laid the sick in the market places and begged
him to let them touch just the tassel of his cloak. All who
touched him got well." (Mk. 6:53-56)*

Let us pray:
0 loving Lord God, how good it is to hear and receive the
message of the good news of your healing power and love.
Thank you for sending us our beloved Jesus Christ who
gently leads us on the path to holiness. Thank you Jesus,
for you have given us much needed hope. You want to reveal God's love for us by healing us of our infirmities and our
sorrows. Our hearts' have been wounded and broken but
through your healing love we are able to be restored and we
turn to you in rejoicing and thanksgiving. Our heavy spirits of
mourning and depression can be changed and transformed
into joyous praise and adoration and our discouragement
can be turned around to positive faith and hopefulness for a
better future. We thank you for restoring health and peace to
our body, mind and soul. Thank you for revealing your true

nature to us. We worship and thank you. Blessed be the name of the Lord now and forever. Amen.

If we are faithful to our daily prayer life we will begin to understand the unlimited power of an all-knowing and holy God. When we pray we are turning to the power of God. There is nothing too difficult for an omnipotent God. *"For nothing is impossible with God." (Lk. 1:37)*

The divine wisdom of God knows and understands all things and will work out whatever the problem is if we are patient and trust. There may be occasions when we are unhappy with the solution because we had our own agenda; however divine wisdom knows something about the situation that we don't. Trusting this higher knowledge is all part and parcel of growing in holiness. We cannot limit the power of God for good in our lives.

Let us pray:
Loving Lord God you are that unlimited love and power that directs our lives. O most gracious and holy one, thank you for blessing us with your goodness. You alone are the holy one. Blessed be the name of the Lord Alleluia, Amen.

A parish priest I know tells his congregation that we are all saints in the making. We must never underestimate the power of grace to transform our lives. I had been going through a great deal of anguish in a particular relationship. I was quite angry with the other person, yet I felt so unhappy and uncomfortable in my anger. I felt justified, yet it upset my thinking and brought havoc into my ordinarily peaceful frame of mind.

I eventually went to God in prayer and asked that the anger I was feeling in my heart be removed. Much to my surprise no sooner did I end the prayer when I felt a

peace and the anger was gone. I marveled at the sudden-
ness of change in my attitude and praised God for such
a miracle. I couldn't even remember what I had been
angry about. I had often tried to be freed from anger
through prayer prior to this but usually it came about
by working it through with some counseling or venting,
or both. Dealing with the anger through forgiveness and
finally letting it go is the usual solution.

I still recommend that anger be worked through with
the help of a mature spiritual guide or counselor. The
power of grace to transform my life was a new lesson I
had to learn in the classroom of holiness. It is through
grace that we can be restored to the peace that passes
all understanding.

Inner peace is a state of being and has the power to
transform our external circumstances. The Holy Spirit
within us is directing us towards the ideals of living life
in peace and we depend on that guidance in all our situations. This is Kingdom living. God is ever-present to
us right here, right now in this very moment. Holiness
dwells within each one of us and is waiting for us to
uncover and discover it as we accept ourselves in the
ordinariness of who we really are, truly human, and beloved of God.

There is a treasure within each one of us. In Holy
Scripture Jesus tells us, *"The reign of God is like a bur-
ied treasure which a man found in a field. He hid it again,
and rejoicing at his find went and sold all he had and
bought that field. (Mt. 13-44)*

Or again, *"The kingdom of heaven is like a merchant's
search for fine pearls. When he found one really valuable
pearl, he went back and put up for sale all that he had
and bought it." (Mt. 13:45-46)* We are that pearl of great
price! We are the treasure!

Let us pray:

O most wondrous and holy God my soul is flooded with the awareness of your divine love. I am surrounded by your infinite, blessed love. Your love, your goodness, your sacredness radiates out from me to all I meet this day and to all who are in my thoughts. You are fully present here with me now in this moment of grace. You O most holy one are that perfect goodness. I am surrounded by your eternal peace and all is well. I no longer fear the past, or the present or the future for you promised to remain with me and in me always. I offer you all my gratitude and praise for you are my ultimate joy and my one true love. Thank you for awakening in me the awareness of your peace and love and the truth of my own holiness. You O loving Lord God are my life. You are unlimited love. You are infinite knowledge. You are the mighty, holy one. I will worship you in spirit and in truth because you are my eternal and loving Lord. Amen.

# Chapter 8

Practicing the Presence of God

Prayers and Exercises for Remaining in the
Presence Of God

Prayer:
Most gracious and loving Lord, help us to respond to your
call of love to us. Our hearts, our minds, our souls yearn for
the peace that only communion with you brings us. We desire the joy of knowing you and living in your presence now
and forever. For this greater grace, we thank you O Lord
God. Amen and Amen.

God is not distant from us. In our ignorance it is we
who distance ourselves from God. Jesus promised that
he would never leave us. He assured us that he would
send an advocate, a Paraclete and a comforter. There is
never a moment of our existence when God is not with
us. After he ascended into heaven, he sent us the Holy
Spirit to be with us always. *"And know that I am with
you always, until the end of the world!" (Mt. 28:20)*

This statement is probably one of the most powerful
in the New Testament sayings of Jesus. If we truly believed and understood that our existence is meaningless
without the real presence of Our Lord and Savior, Jesus
Christ then we would also have to concede that there is

no need to be worried or anxious about the future.

The more we become aware and practice the presence of God's eternal love on a moment to moment basis; we will eventually become accustomed to being in a state of oneness with the Divine source of our life. God is always accessible to us. We need but awaken from the nightmare of this worlds' belief in separation.

Scripture also instructs us to 'put on the mind of Christ. *"The Spirit we have received is not the world spirit but God's Spirit, helping us to recognize the gifts he has given us. We speak of these, not in words of human wisdom but in words taught by the Spirit thus interpreting spiritual things in spiritual terms. The natural man does not accept what is taught by the Spirit of God, for him that is absurdity. He cannot come to know such teaching because it must be appraised in a spiritual way. The spiritual man on the other hand, can appraise everything, though he himself can be appraised by no one. For who has known the mind of the Lord so as to instruct him? But we have the mind of Christ."* (1 Cor. 2:12-16)

In the early years of my spiritual journey I made it a habit of rising early in the morning to spend some time in silent prayer, then see my five children off to school. After that I would attend daily Mass. Even after my children were long grown and gone from the nest this routine became a part of my daily life to this day. As Catholics we believe that Jesus is truly present in Holy Communion. The Church also offers us special days of adoration where we may enjoy the Presence of Jesus in the Holy Eucharist, usually in a Monstrance on the altar followed by Benediction.

### Silent Prayer
In those early years of learning how to pray I often struggled with silent prayer. There were moments during and

after prayer where I would experience Gods' presence in a very real and sometimes emotional way. I would feel consoled, comforted, peaceful and loved. Just as often I might sit in the quiet and experience nothing at all.

During this interval I would get edgy, agitated and then shy away from the practice for a while and try again later. I continued in this vein for a number of years, gradually expanding my times of silent prayer from sitting still in the morning hours to various times during the day when I felt the need to do so.

I usually put a great deal of effort into it, making a project out of it. I was intent on doing it perfectly and thought, "one of these day I will get it right." Perfectionism played a role and was just one of my character defects that had to be dealt with eventually. Mother Theresa of the Sisters of Charity in Calcutta, India gave a statement that can sum up the need to find the silence I was trying so hard to attain.

"We need to find God, and God cannot be found in noise and restlessness. God is the friend of silence. See how nature...trees, flowers, grass grows in silence; see the stars, the moon and the sun, how they move in silence...We need silence to be able to touch souls." Mother Theresa

The movie, "Take the Lead," is about inner-city teenagers in a high school learning ballroom dancing in order to enter a state-wide contest. The two lead teenagers were practicing their steps when the young man, observing his partner, pauses to remark to her, "You seem to be at peace while we are dancing." She replies, "I'm in my moment...In the silence I can forget my worries."

Artists have told me that there is a point in their creativity when they are in the "zone," that is, "in the moment," or "in the quiet."

It finally took a serious illness for me to realize and fully understand that the God of Love I was searching for is in every moment. Scripture tells us, "In Him we live and move and have our being. (Acts 17-28)

*"Silence, all mankind, in the presence of the Lord!"* (Zec. 217)

In the early months of January to July of 1984 I discovered a large lump in my left breast. The results of a mammogram revealed a three and a half to four inch tumor with eighty percent of my breast tissue affected. The prognosis indicated a ninety five percent certainty it was carcinoma.

Once the initial shock wore off I went into prayer for guidance. Against the recommendations of the medical profession, I chose to seek out alternative solutions. I refused a biopsy for reasons of my own. This upset many friends and family and try as they did, no one could talk me out of my decision.

I would never suggest to anyone else that they try this method, unless they were convinced as I was that this was the way for me to be cured. At this time I had already been living to some extent a deep spiritual life and had been in a full time healing prayer ministry as well. I was used to praying with countless people for the healing of many life-threatening illnesses.

I had experienced first hand the awesomeness of God's love and felt quite strongly that the condition I found myself in was asking me to trust more deeply in the mystery of that love. This is not to say that I was without a great deal of fear and had bouts of anxiety.

Within me was  a mixture of confusion, conviction, surrender to God and super vigilance as well as a heightened awareness of Gods' presence at any given moment. As I look back on that amazing event I have no doubt I was led by the power and grace of The Holy Spirit. The Holy Spirit is the presence of Jesus here on earth. I cried out to heaven for help and I extend my humble and sincere gratitude to those blessed intercessors from the beyond, the Healing Saints and Angels and of course our beloved Mother Mary.

During the days and weeks following the results of the mammogram I began to immerse myself in exploring the ways in which I could access God's holy presence. In hindsight I know it was a wonderful opportunity for me to learn how to practice the presence of God in my daily life.

I did not rely on scheduled times of prayer, rather I began to prepare for the healing I needed by taking more time to be in the silence and listen. It was a challenge, although I'm sure I was not consciously aware of it, since I was acting out of a primitive survival mode, and felt I could only trust the one true source of my life for the problem I faced.

I believed at this point that too many people throughout my life had abandoned me. I felt instinctively that Jesus was my one and true and only real friend. I needed to draw closer to him as much as I needed to breathe. Jesus was my lifeline. In reflecting back and realizing how far I had come in trusting God for my healing, it was extraordinary. God had planted seeds in my soul and I was prepared to receive the nurturing and caring love that would bring about a deeper and more significant transformation of my mind, soul and spirit.

Since I felt different from other people, it was a lonely time. I have learned from others since then, that this is a common feeling among those faced with the experience of a life-threatening illness. In spite of what I was feeling many of my close spiritual friends supported me with encouragement and love even though they were concerned as to whether I had made the right decision. I appreciated their sincere desire to be of help to me.

There were many times when I felt a deep intimacy with the Lord and my feelings of loneliness dissipated and the clouds disappeared. During this time I com-

posed a simple poem...
    Love is being Present:
    Love is being present when I am lonely...Love is being
    present when I am sad...
    Love is being present when I am glad...Love is being
    present when I need someone...to listen to my ideas.
    Love is being present when I need someone... to listen
    to my fears.
    Love is being present to who I am...
    Without judgment. Love is being present.


In the world of practicality, I participated in my healing
in various activities that would aid me along the way. I
went to a therapist/counselor each week in order to work
on my negative attitudes and feelings. I found I needed
to forgive a great many people from my childhood.

    Forgiveness was probably the most significant part of
my healing process. I began exercising which I always
found to be tedious but decided to take long walks in
nature several times a day, New York weather permit-
ting of course. I consulted a nutritionist and embarked
on healthier and natural ways of eating along with vita-
mins and herbs. I asked believing friends whom I trusted to pray for me and with me.

    Never had I considered how much I was loved by oth-
ers until these dear friends reached out to me during
this fearful episode of my life. The problem that constantly plagued me during this period was a nagging
and unrelenting fear of the disease. My therapist suggested that when I let go of my anxiety about it, then I
would be cured.

    My constant guide and teacher...The Holy Spirit re-
minded me to focus on what I truly believed about God's
unconditional love for me. I worked on thinking about
God and all the attributes associated with God. When-

ever the ugly head of fear would appear and I was tempted to become panic-stricken I would be reminded to stop and sit and be silent and reflect on some aspect of God. Such as; *"God is love,"* *(1Jn. 4:8)* and *"Perfect love casts out all fear." (1Jn. 4:18)*

I became actively involved in focusing on acknowledging the greatness and goodness of God's love. The light of God's love gradually overcame the darkness of my fears. But it took time and patience.

> Let us pray:
> Loving Lord God, shed your radiant light upon the shadow of my fears. Pour forth your luminous light upon the darkness of my mind and help me to see more clearly the beauty of your love. Help me never to lose sight of your caring concern for my well-being. Lord Jesus you are the light of the world and I thank you for shining your endless light upon me. Amen.

I made a decision to discipline myself and set up a program, playing inspirational music to calm myself, preparing my mind to receive. Then I would sit and be still, quieting my mind and begin to think about all I knew God to be. It was important to me to focus on God's perfect love and that I was truly loved.

I needed reassurance that I was loved by God. I relied on Holy Scripture for claims that would assure me. *"Love has no room for fear, rather perfect love casts our all fear." (1Jn. 4:18)*

I reflected on particular verses of scripture and repeated them like a mantra over and over to myself. *"Perfect love casts out all fear."* After repeating the verses it would generally lead me to an affirmation such as, "I am in the presence of perfect love. There is nothing to fear."

I repeated various phrases over and over. Eventually

my anxiety would abate and I would be at peace again. I would use this exercise often because my fears were a constant source of concern to me. When I became troubled again, I would stop whatever I was doing, sit in the silence and focus my awareness on words that would remind me of God's loving presence. The Holy Spirit was my constant guide and teacher.

All throughout this time I was being given valuable lessons in regards to love and forgiveness. There is an ancient saying that practice makes perfect. There is simply no significant achievement without practice as any accomplished musician will tell you. True spirituality may well be summed up as a movement of God's grace in every given moment. This grace is the answer to our despair for in it is the greatest and purest love we can ever know.

The object of all this work was to expel the fears I felt and exchange them by substituting positive and holy thoughts. This process helped me tremendously. Before I go any further I would like you to know there was a happy ending to my story.

In July of 1984, six months after the diagnosis, I decided it was time for another mammogram. The results finally came in after waiting for a few weeks. When I went to get the outcome the technicians were puzzled by what they saw when they compared the current with the first set of X-Rays.

They questioned me as to what form of medication had been recommended. When I told them that I took no medication but went the route of healing prayer, and alternative therapies they looked at me thoughtfully, hesitated and then left the room keeping me waiting for quite some time.

On the form they presented to me in silence were written the words, "a striking resolution of mass." In other words the tumor and the resulting tissue damage were completely gone. Of course without a biopsy we will never know if it was cancer. The important factor was that it was gone and I was given valuable information that helped transform my life.

The greatest lesson I learned was to trust in God's ultimate goodness and kindness. Those six months were a training ground in awakening in me knowledge that God will never be separated from me. *"Awake, O sleeper, arise from the dead, and Christ will give you light." (Eph. 5:14)*

Separation can only happen in my mind when I believe that my wrong actions can create a chasm in my relationship with God. The lesson I learned first and foremost was that God is always there with me.

Unfortunately for many, the belief system so prevalent in our society thinks that God is out there, up there, somewhere. My prayer is that all God's people will discover that God is closer than the breath we breathe. God is present in our working, studying, playing, eating, resting or exercising. *"Seek first the kingdom of God and all these things will be added to you." (Lk. 12:31)*

Let us pray:
Loving Lord God, help be to become more aware of your loving presence regardless of where I am or what I am doing. Free me from the inhibitions of adulthood and restore my sense of spontaneity and freedom of spirit. Free me from the fears that keep me separated from you. Lead me into the center of your heart of love, the holy of holies where peace and joy abide and heal me of the blocks to the awareness of your love. Help me to live in your presence always. Blessed be your holy name now and forever. Amen.

Another form of worship that helps us in practicing the Presence of God has to include praise and thanksgiving.

The Catholic reference Dictionary defines prayer as the voluntary response to the awareness of God's Presence.

This response may be an acknowledgement of God's greatness and of a person's total dependence on him, (adoration). Or gratitude for benefits received and others, (thanksgiving).

As a child I attended Catholic schools and the nuns would usually put short prayers or reflections on the blackboard for us to memorize. It was in a way teaching us to remember Our Lord during the day.

Of course once we left the classroom we hardly ever gave it another thought. I guess I should speak for myself. We were taught for example:

"Sacred Heart of Jesus, I place my trust in Thee."...

"Immaculate Heart of Mary pray for us." ...

"Jesus, Mary and Joseph pray for us."

I was to find, in spite of myself, that they were not wasted on me, for many times when I am in distress I will recall these prayers and automatically say, "Jesus, help me, or Sacred Heart of Jesus I place my trust in you."

Every Friday in Catholic grade school the nuns would lead us to the Church where we would experience the liturgy of the Exposition of the Blessed Sacrament and Benediction.

This was a sacred time and I recall the sense of reverence and holiness associated with this event. It remains my favorite form of worship to this present day. My home life and childhood years were bleak to say the least, but the one blazing light of peace I felt at that time was during the exposition of the beautiful golden Monstrance and the precious Blessed Sacrament in the center of the Altar surrounded by brilliant candlelight.

During that one hour each week, kneeling in the silence, I felt consoled, safe and at peace. There was a bit of humor in all of this. In that school I attended, the boys were separated from the girls and sat on the right hand side of the Church with the girls on the left to avoid distraction. At the end of Benediction we always sang "Holy God we Praise Thy Name. Lord of all we bow before Thee."

The boys' voices of course had not developed yet and there was this unspoken competition where the boys and the girls would try to see who could sing the loudest. I recall seeing one of the nuns suppressing a smile.

Before the end of Benediction we recited the "Divine Praises." Recited to this day wherever Benediction is performed they are ingrained in my memory: Blessed be God...Blessed be his Holy Name...Blessed be Jesus Christ, true God and true man...Blessed be the name of Jesus...Blessed be his most Sacred Heart...Blessed be His most Precious Blood...Blessed be Jesus in the most Holy Sacrament of the altar...Blessed be the Holy Spirit, the Paraclete.

Blessed be the great Mother of God, Mary most holy...Blessed be her holy and Immaculate Conception... Blessed be her glorious Assumption. Blessed be St. Joseph, her most chaste Spouse. Blessed be God in His Angels and in His Saints. The Divine Praises accentuated devotion to Our Lord, Our Blessed Mother, Mary and the Saints in heaven.

We had a rich treasury of prayers and mysticism to draw from in the Church. The nuns also taught us to pray the 'Hail Mary' whenever we would hear a fire engine or police siren in the distance passing by the school. To this day whenever I hear an ambulance or fire engine I still remember to say this prayer. "Hail Mary full of Grace the Lord is with you. Blessed are you among women and blessed is the fruit of your womb, Jesus. Holy Mary, Mother of God, pray for us sinners now and at the hour of our death. Amen."

After I received the good news of my healing, I went about praising God and continued my daily practices of silent prayer. Many opportunities to practice forgiveness presented themselves on a daily basis. I continued using affirmations, but my motivation for doing so had changed.

I thought that I had wanted to embrace a deeper knowledge of God's presence so that I could be cured and also so that I could be a more effective instrument in helping other people. It was an attempt at bargaining with God and I'm willing to admit that God was probably amused by it.

I realize now that all my efforts were just preparing the soil to open my soul to the wondrous compassion Our Lord has for me. Practicing the presence and being aware of God in every aspect of my life is just good common sense. From the time I arise in the morning and all through the day it helps me to know I am loved, protected and guided in making right decisions by a real and loving presence.

Morning Prayer:
Most eternal and Loving Lord God I turn my life and my will over to your care this day. I believe you to be a God of unconditional love and overflowing joy. I surrender this day to you, and thank you for this brand new day...a day that has never been lived before. I pray and ask that everything I say and do today be guided, inspired and directed by the power of the Holy Spirit. If it is not meant to be said or done, place a seal over my lips and a block in my path. I pray that only those thoughts, words and actions that pour forth from the throne of God's grace be manifested through me today. I pray that I am in the right place at exactly the right time. I ask for your protection, health and salvation for all my loved ones, family and friends as well as for myself. Let it be done by the power of the Holy Spirit and in the holy name of Our

Lord and Savior, Jesus Christ. Amen.

There are times when I feel down hearted and I just don't know why and I will ask to be shown God's love during the day. The answer will usually come unexpectedly by someone saying something kind to me, giving me a smile or a word of encouragement. It may happen that I will hear from someone I had not heard from in a long while and they wanted me know they were thinking of me. Sometimes it is so personal I just know it had to have come from the Holy Spirit.

Many years ago, when I was a young mother, I sent my five children off to catch the school bus. After they left, I said out loud, "I think I would like a nice cold glass of orange juice." Alas the juice carton was empty. I shrugged it off and went about straightening up the house and just going about my morning chores.

About twenty minutes later, a neighbor knocked on the side door that opened into my kitchen. She had been at the supermarket shopping when the thought came to her to buy me a half-gallon of orange juice. I was absolutely amazed! Astounded! To this day I am still in awe. My neighbor and friend, Rinda Sternberg, had no idea that I needed orange juice. Who would have thought that the Holy Spirit was interested in supplying a young housewife with orange juice?

Back in those days I desperately needed, wanted and yearned to know if God cared about me personally and here was the proof. I knew Rinda to be a prayerful Christian woman who never left her home without saying her morning prayers.

A heavenly messenger heard my little request and then quickly whispered in her ear at the supermarket and so she heard and acted upon it. Such a little thing made such a difference in the life of this young mother who carried so much pain and abandonment from her childhood.

It is important for us to follow through on our intuitions and our good intentions because we might otherwise miss an opportunity to make a difference in someone's life. We will never know how God will fill our need because divine love knows about it even before we do.

Experiences such as this naturally give reason for amazement and gratitude for God's loving kindness. God is so good! *"My God in turn will supply your needs fully, in a way worthy of his magnificent riches in Christ Jesus. All glory to our God for unending ages! Amen." (Phil. 4:19)..."Truly the light shines in the darkness and darkness has not overcome it" (Jn. 1:5)*

One day as I was taking a walk and pondering the goodness of God, this thought came to me... "I am because God is. I am because God is." I considered what this must mean and came to the conclusion that the reality for me now is to know that I am loved just because I exist. *"Truly in Him, I live and move and have my being." (Acts 17:28)*

"Help" is probably the best prayer we can ever say when we need it. Humility recognizes that we can do nothing of ourselves and that all is "gift" flowing out from a bountiful and providential Creator. The psalms are also a wonderful source of comfort. *"Even though I may walk in a dark valley I will fear no evil for God is with me, God is at my side." (Psalm 23:4)... "God is our refuge and our strength, an ever present help in distress." (Psalm 46:1)* ...Jesus reminds us, *"Know that I am with you always until the end of the world."* (Mt. 28.20)

The reality is that we are never alone. God is always present in each moment. Each day is a new holy day where we remind ourselves once again that God is with us. This day we rise and meet Our Lord in prayer and gratitude, thankful that we have been given the grace to know and experience the peace that surpasses all understanding. We possess a Love above all others. *"The Lord is my light and my salvation; whom should I fear? The Lord is my life's refuge; of whom should I be afraid?"(Psalm 27:1)* Right here, right now I will not be afraid!

## The Practice of Holy Thoughts

This exercise in the practice of holy thoughts is meant to help us focus on the awareness of God's presence. We are not trying to reach God as though "he" were out there somewhere, but rather to achieve a state of stillness so that we become aware of God's presence within us. Contemplative prayer is a tool that enables us to quiet ourselves and can become a way of life if we practice it on a regular basis.

When a person is learning how to practice stillness it is essential to prepare a comfortable place to be in and begin by relaxing the body. Using a meditation recording is helpful or repeating positive phrases such as... "I am relaxed...every muscle, every nerve, every cell, every atom of my body is relaxing."

Try repeating this and place your attention on your toes, wiggling them and flexing them. Release and let go... "My toes are relaxed. My feet and ankles are relaxed, etc." This exercise can be used by focusing your attention on all the components of the body using the same method.

Taking deep breaths by inhaling into the diaphragm and eventually bringing the breath down into the belly and releasing slowly through the mouth is helpful in learning to relax. Breathe and relax. All the way up the body to the back of the head and scalp, saying..."My head, my scalp are relaxed now."

Breathe in and out and let go of all burdens and concerns and repeat affirming messages such as "I let go and let God...I am in God's loving hands...I am at peace, etc." There are many meditation methods that are helpful in aiding us in the art of relaxing and learning how to still the body. This is not easy and takes time and patience with oneself especially if you have an active mind and life. But it is important to remember to stay with it. Just do it.

Repeat the following affirmations three times slowly:

> Where I am God is
> God is perfect love
> The love of God enfolds me
> In God I live and move and have my being.
> The Lord is God there is no other

> God is eternal light
> Light from light, true God from true God
> The light of Christ fills my life with purpose
> The healing light of Christ flows throughout every atom of my being
> The Lord is my light and my salvation, whom should I fear

> The Lord is my strength, my stronghold
> I am in God's loving hands
> I am God's holy creation
> The Lord helps me in my need
> In stillness and in peace I receive the gift of love

> Jesus came that I might have life and have it more abundantly
> I choose to live life to the fullest
> The fullness of joy is my inheritance as a child of God
> I have faith in God's promise to be with me always

God's grace is sufficient to meet my every need

I receive the gift of The Holy Spirit
The Spirit of the living God restores me, body, mind
and spirit
My entire being is filled with peace and health by the
power of the Holy Spirit
I am blessed beyond measure
I am thankful to my gracious and generous God

Consciousness or being aware is vital in this process of awakening to the Presence of God within us. Whenever we make the effort to be aware of God we are in the Kingdom of God. The core of our being is holy ground. God is in us and we are in God no matter where we are.

I was very fortunate to have many spiritual mentors during my years of spiritual growth. One advised me to take up journaling. Writing down on paper our feelings and thoughts helps to guide us by bringing us to an awareness of what we are experiencing or thinking about our spiritual walk.

God speaks to us in many different ways and journaling can be a source of listening to what God is trying to convey to us. Very often in the silence, thoughts and ideas we never dreamed of suddenly seem to surface. In a sense it can be a dialogue with our soul.

I was often able to tap into unresolved and repressed anger and unforgiveness. On paper I was able to express my pain and sorrow as well as my joys and new found expressions of love and peace. Through this medium I often could write down my feelings about God and write my gratitude and praise that welled up from within me.

Keeping a notebook for this purpose was helpful and when I would read what I had written after some years I saw how I had grown in the spiritual life. It is keeping a spiritual diary in a sense. The writing down of our thoughts and feelings helps us to turn within where the Spirit of God dwells and once again we can return to a place of presence.

We all need to know we are loved and that we are valued for who we are. *"Who will separate us from the love of Christ? For I am certain that neither death, nor life, neither angels nor principalities, neither the present nor the future, nor powers, neither height nor depth nor any other creature will be able to separate us from the love of God that comes to us in Christ Jesus, our Lord." (Rom. 35-39)*

Practicing the presence of God is a work in practicing stillness and quiet. *"Be still and know that I am God."* *(Psalm 46:10)*

In quiet times of prayer we will eventually discover the mystery unfolding within us. This life we live belongs to God, our Creator and Redeemer. What we do with this life is our choice since God has been so gracious in giving us freedom to choose. We have been given the present moment, this moment to live in the Kingdom of God.

<u>Prayer of Devotion to the Eternal Presence of the Most High and Glorious God:</u>
O most gracious and loving and glorious God, I humbly enter into your eternal Presence, aware of my frailties and temptations. I place myself before the throne of your grace, where your eternal love is brilliantly shining. I need your cleansing love to heal me as I place my pain and unforgiveness before you. Help me to surrender all my faults to your loving kindness. O Blessed Lord God there is none like you. There is no one here on earth that knows and understands me as you do. There is no one else who can see my distress. You are the only one I can cast my cares and concerns and worries upon. I think I am carrying burdens that are too hard for me to bear. All too often I feel alone, abandoned and

separated from you. I call to you in my need and thank you that you are listening. I know that only you can satisfy the desires of my heart and the hunger and thirst that are within my soul. Whenever I have called out to you in the past you have always been there for me, helping me, guiding me, and instructing me. Whenever I have felt in danger you have protected me and I become aware of your presence. Thank you for the mighty angels who surround me as I go about my daily life. Your holy presence restores my faith and my heart rejoices that I have so great a love beyond compare. This world will pass away but in your holy presence I am assured of the joy of Heaven in this present moment for you are with me. O Lord, my God I praise and adore you for you are my solace, my comforter, my redeemer. You are the holy one. You are my God and there is no other. Blessed be your greatness and goodness now and forever! Amen!

Father Peter McCall

# Chapter 9

Remembrances of Father Peter McCall, OFM, CAP.
1935-2001

## The Champion of the Lenient Opinion

I dedicate this chapter to Franciscan Capuchin Priest, Father Peter McCall. Promoting forgiveness and non-violence as a way of life became his mission and passion during the many years I worked with him. While a young seminarian, one of his instructors labeled him "the champion of the lenient opinion." Father Peter often used this phrase—the champion of the lenient opinion—to describe himself. His life and his works reflect the true meaning of those words.

I met Father Peter McCall in the spring of 1978 at a time when I was feeling overwhelmed by the events that led me to believe God was calling me to a healing ministry. Father Peter was at a crossroads in his life and was contemplating where the Lord was leading him. He had been in the missions in the South Pacific for many years and had returned to New York. We both were going through major transitions in our lives. Therefore it is with some amazement to me how the powers of heaven set in motion the union of our souls and minds to be coworkers in spreading the good news of Gods' healing love for well over twenty years.

We had within our hearts a profound love and zeal for the healing message of Jesus Christ. Embarking on this journey together we had no doubt our ministry was ordained by God. The many hours we spent before the Blessed Sacrament in prayer helped us to grow intuitively in that God was calling us to serve hurt and wounded people of the Church.

One day after prayer, Father Peter opened his Bible to this passage: "... if this endeavor or this activity is of human origin, it will destroy itself. If, on the other hand, it comes from God, you will not be able to destroy it without fighting against God himself, (Acts 5:28-39). (NAB)

Throughout the years (1979-2001) we worked together, the fruits of that scripture passage were manifested in the many thousands of people we served through The House of Peace, the healing center which we cofounded and those we ministered to at healing Masses, services, retreats and pilgrimages held throughout the U.S. and the Caribbean as well as in Mexico, Canada, Europe and the Holy Land.

My intention is to keep alive the inspiring thoughts and ideas, which Father Peter shared. Those of us who knew him believed his teachings were way ahead of their time and that his thoughtful insights of God's unconditional love helped to educate and liberate many. People were attracted to him because of his down to earth approach to life. Humble and non judgmental Peter McCall accepted everyone just as they were. I didn't fully understand his spirituality in the beginning of our friendship, until I worked with him and observed how Christ-like he tried to be.

An excerpt from his writings include: "Tenderness is a way of non-violence which we constantly have to work at and learn. Tenderness does not come automatically to minds which are accustomed to violence and attack.

Tenderness takes training."

A major inner healing of my life came about as a result of his patience and kindness. Because of my childhood issues where violence and attack were everyday occurrences I had been apprehensive of men in general.

Whenever a misunderstanding arose between us in the years we worked together, Peter McCall would approach me and offer to discuss it in order that we may understand each other better and restore peace. He was inclined to listen to the problem with sincerity and gentleness and try to come to reconciliation and a peaceful solution. When a confrontation was addressed in this way, an enormous level of deeper healing transpired within me.

The way I would have dealt with a similar issue in the past would be to just close him out rather than communicate, the main and important reason being that I truly expected a hostile and defensive run-in.

Resentment and avoidance was how I was used to playing out a difficult relationship problem. With Peter McCall it was totally the opposite from what I expected because he met me with consideration and respect for my feelings.

When I share this experience with others, I find that many women are just as amazed as I was because communication on this level was not the usual in our dealing with the average male, whether as a spouse or in a friendship.

It took me a number of years to figure out that I hadn't perceived Father Peter McCall as a partner. I saw him as an authority figure and the amazing gift was that he saw me as his equal. My perception eventually changed.

In time we came to a mutual understanding of minds and became the dearest of friends. It was indeed a miracle of grace!

I will be eternally grateful to God for the gift of Fa-

ther Peter McCall, OFM, Cap., and for the opportunity
of working on a highly spiritual level with this precious
man. He knew my soul as no other could.

My heart broke when he died suddenly at the age of
sixty-five of a major heart attack in March 2001. I was
left bereft and the sense of loss was unfathomable.

He left us a wonderful legacy in his writings, homilies and teachings. My most vivid memories of him are
of his working at his desk studying and writing. When
I would appear at the healing center in the morning he
would have been there from the early morning hours
and would be deep in thought and reflection.

After his death I came across a multitude of note-
books filled with his writings. He loved issuing random
"one-liners" to his listeners such as:

- "The past is forgiveness, the future is providence
  and the present is God indwelling.
- "We cannot prevent God's love from shining on us,
  but we can prevent it from shining through us."
- "Our thoughts will come and go but the Presence
  of God remains with me always."
- "God is always near us because God is within us."
- "We live in eternity now, so what's the hurry. Se-
  renity is never in a rush."
- "The time to relax is when you don't have time to
  do it."
- "People need love the most when they least de-
  serve it."
- "We do not stop playing when we grow old; we
  grow old when we stop playing."
- "The question is not, is there life after death, but
  is there life before death."
- "We are not loved because we are good; we are
  good because we are loved."
- "There is no "they," only "us.""

A good friend of ours, James Gannon approached me after Father Peter's death and offered to transcribe some of his taped homilies to print. I realized what a big contribution this was and so I include them in this remembrance of a remarkable Priest. These homilies were recorded on a series of audio-cassettes relating to "The Wisdom Sayings of Jesus."

## Jesus-Himself

A Homily by Fr. Peter McCall OFM,
Cap. Feast of the Epiphany
*(Transcribed from audio)*

This is a last segment in a series on the wisdom of Jesus. What I would like to do this time, this last of the series, is to simply speak about my favorite topic, JESUS, Himself.

If we have said anything, we said that there is no substitute for a personal relationship with Jesus. This is the heart and soul of our religion and it's the heart and soul of our spiritual life and that is to be intimate with Jesus.

Like God, Jesus has been misunderstood and there are distortions about him. One reason is because we have no record that Jesus himself ever wrote anything. The only instance of his writing is in the story of the woman caught in adultery (Re: Jn. 8:3-11). We're told that Jesus bent down and wrote on the ground. This is the only indication in the Gospels that Jesus ever wrote anything.

There are books and books written on the question of what did Jesus write in the dirt? Some Scripture scholars suggest that he wrote down the sins of the people who were condemning the woman because it says they took a look and then they gradually began to walk away.

This leads to a distortion about Jesus because in those days they didn't have video tapes or audio tapes. We don't have the exact words of Jesus and we have to rely on the evangelists who had to remember, thirty or forty years later, facts about Jesus. (And when you have a writer you are going to get some of his prejudices or where he his coming from.)

So, we have to sift through the Gospels because Matthew, Mark, Luke and John have written four completely different accounts of the life of Jesus. They are all telling us about Jesus but from their own perspective. So, we have to look for what we call the overwhelming message of Jesus because sometimes that message is going to be like a big fish story.

Every time the story is told the fish gets a little bit bigger. It's basically the same thing with the stories about Jesus. They sometimes get a little bit exaggerated, especially if the evangelist wants to make a point. Sometimes they put words in the mouth of Jesus, which we know from the overwhelming message of Jesus, that Jesus simply did not say which I will speak about later.

The first news I have to tell you is that the historians think that Jesus must have been Irish. After all, He was thirty years old and not married. He lived with his Mother. He was not gainfully employed, and his Mother thought he was God. (Laughter)

One of the mistakes, I suppose the most important one, that was made about Jesus was the one the Jews themselves made. One of the reasons why they did not recognize the Messiah when he came was because they had this image of the Messiah as a political savior, that is, someone who was going to come in the spirit of David and be an earthly king.

As a result, when Jesus did come as a spiritual Savior, to free us from our sins, they missed him because they had a wrong idea of what the Messiah was to be. Jesus had come as a covenant to save us from our sins, which is what God had promised.

The Jews weren't the only ones to make this mistake. We make it every time we see in Jesus as someone who is going to save us from our enemies, someone who is going to be a political savior for our country, our race or our neighborhood.

In other words, once we believe that Jesus is on our side and we are on the side of Jesus, we think we are the good guys. Therefore, those people out there are the bad guys so we use the name of Jesus to justify separation, alienation, prejudice and this is where we have a distorted image of Jesus.

It's been done in the past and it is still being done. We know that during the time of the Crusades they had a saying, "Kill a Turk for Jesus." In the name of Jesus, there were killings during the Inquisition, justifying violence and murder. Anytime Jesus is used to uphold a political party or a particular belief we are saying that he is an earthly king.

However, in the Gospel when Jesus was standing before Pilate, he said very clearly, "My kingdom is not of this world." He was very firm about this. He separated himself from politics when he was asked about paying taxes to Caesar. His response was, "Give to Caesar, what belongs to Caesar, but give to God what belongs to God."

He is telling us not to use his name to justify anything in politics where you set yourself up as right and someone else is wrong because that is not why Jesus came to this earth.

The overwhelming message of Jesus is universal. That is what this feast of the Epiphany is all about. Jesus came for all people and not just a certain elite club.

Jesus is the Savior of the whole world. His universal message of salvation is extremely important in that He is everyone's Savior.

Some theologians say that there is no indication that Jesus ever intended to set up a particular church. In fact in the encyclopedia under The Catholic Church...it will say it was founded by St. Paul.

Jesus had nothing to do with setting up a hierarchy. Jesus was a Rabbi, a teacher of God and a healer. He came to bring good news to all the people and to let them know that their sins have been forgiven.

The church was established by the early Christians and by St. Paul. He was the one that set up Bishops and Presbyters. Scripture scholars say that it seems as if Jesus had no intention of founding a separate church apart from or in opposition to Judaism.

That was done after him. If you want to look at it from a historical point of view, Jesus had nothing to do with that. It was done by his followers.

My brothers and sisters, when a charismatic figure like Jesus comes on the scene and has a message from God that is valid, and performs miracles of healing and then leaves the scene, it's usually the followers that distort it.

We know this from the life of St. Francis of Assisi. When you read the life of St. Francis you see he is as free as a bird. While St. Francis was around everything was fine. After St. Francis died, in came the institution and in came forms and regimentation which St. Francis never had in mind!

When St. Francis traveled to see the Pope, saying he wanted to found an order, he was told he had to have a rule. So St. Francis sat down and wrote a series of Gospel statements. He said this was his rule and the life of the Friars Minor was to observe the holy Gospel of Our Lord Jesus Christ.

He handed that to the Pope and the Pope said "This is no rule. You cannot keep this!" Francis looked at him and said, "You mean we can't keep the Gospel of Jesus Christ? That's all I want to do is to follow the Gospel."

When we begin to talk about the injustices of the church we are not talking about Jesus. Jesus is somewhat separate from the organizational church. Even the kingdom of God is not the church.

St. Augustine has been known to say, "God has people that the church does not have and the church has people that God doesn't have." So, again we have be very clear when we speak about Jesus, that we are speaking about someone who brought us a universal message of salvation for all the people for all time.

The second point about Jesus is that we sometimes use Him to justify religious abuse. Sometimes we use the name of Jesus, the teachings of Jesus and the church of Jesus to manipulate and control people.

The way this is accomplished is by making them feel guilty. So things are said like "God is out to get you, or Jesus is not pleased with you, or Jesus sees everything you do." Jesus is then used as a weapon to control and manipulate others.

This is religious abuse. If Jesus ever came to do anything, as John the Baptist pointed him out and said, "There is the lamb of God who is going to take away sin." When sin is taken away, the guilt is removed. This was the mission of Jesus here on earth, to free us from sin and to free us from guilt.

Yet people try to use the very name of Jesus to promote guilt and make people feel worse. This is distorting the message of Jesus because Jesus came to take away our sin and take away our guilt, not to heap more guilt upon us. He doesn't want to make us feel more miserable or guilty.

The third point I want to make is a big one. That is

to use Jesus to justify victim-hood. My dear brothers and sisters, Jesus was no victim. Now I know, that in the Gospels of Matthew, Mark and Luke, the synoptic Gospels, their approach to Jesus was presenting him as the suffering servant in Isaiah.

They give the impression and portrayed a passive Jesus as the suffering servant. By the time John writes his Gospel, he is correcting that theory. In John's Gospel, especially Jn. 8:18, Jesus says, *"No one takes my life from me. I lay it down on my own."*

In John's Gospel, you see Jesus is always in charge. He is never portrayed as a passive victim. Jesus never said to anyone who came to him for healing, "why don't you offer it up, or offer your sufferings up."

This was a spirituality that came after Jesus so it is not authentic Jesus spirituality. The authentic spirituality of Jesus revealed that he healed everyone who came to him. Everyone who touched him in faith, Jesus healed.

In the Gospel of John, Jesus was no victim and He knew what he was doing all the time. When they tried to kill him, he would say things like, "My time has not yet come," and he would simply disappear. Jesus knew what he was doing, he knew the will of his Father, and what he was going to do and no one was going to take that from him.

Jesus never said, "Oh well, I'm just a poor victim. I'm a victim, and I can't do anything about what is going on around me." No! That is not the authentic message of the spirituality of Jesus.

Thank God for St. Matthew's Sermon on the Mount. The two things in the Gospels that we can rely on are: The Sermon on the Mount, and the Parables of Jesus.

Sometimes we cannot count on the interpretation of the Parables, but they were the way that Jesus taught. It is an abuse of Scripture when we interpret literally, what

Jesus meant metaphorically.

For example, Jesus would never intend anyone to cut off their hand or pluck out their eye and yet people have taken that Scripture literally and have done so. Yet some will say it's in Scripture. No. It's a distortion. As a teacher, I may speak in a way of metaphor, but it is not to be taken literally.

Sometimes it is easy to tell where the Evangelist is putting his own words in the mouth of Jesus, because it is so contrary to the overwhelming message of Jesus, that we know Jesus would never have said that.

For example: In Matthew's Gospel, Jesus is supposed to have said of Judas, "That it would have been better had he not been born." Another example, "It is better that a person have a millstone tied around their neck and be thrown into the depths of the sea."

Another example, "Do not think, I have come to bring peace, I have come to bring the sword." When you read this or hear this, if you have any relationship with Jesus, you know that someone is putting those words in the mouth of Jesus.

Another thing that you need to be aware of is back in those days, there were no printing presses. Everything was written by hand and it was a difficult thing to do. They wrote on leaves with watercolors. It would fade very soon, so it had to be written again and again.

It eventually became the work of the monks and it was all written by hand. Well, obviously, if you look at the various versions of the Bible, you will see that some monks added some things.

A good example is the Our Father. "For Thine is the Kingdom and the Power and the Glory" was added and it has been handed down from one generation to the next. This has been accepted but we have to begin to think about, what did Jesus really say?

The only way it can be discerned, is by looking at his

overwhelming message of love, his message of peace and if it doesn't seem to fit, we can say, "wait a minute now." The Jesus of the Sermon on the Mount would never have said that.

This is an important point so that we don't go around using Jesus to justify some of the sad things that we do in life.

My next point here is to show how so many people tend to picture Jesus without a sense of humor and that everyone around him was somber and serious. Therefore this false image of Jesus justifies all kinds of austerities and bodily penances.

You will have people like the Flagellants, the people who scourge themselves, and do all kinds of severe things in the name of Jesus. They somehow think or picture him as being pleased when we are miserable.

Fortunately in our day we have been seeing pictures of the smiling Jesus. It has to be understood that no austere, morbid person could attract the crowds that Jesus attracted.

He must have had a tremendous personality. He must have been able to laugh and be joyful. Look at all the times he spent with publicans and sinners. You don't think he was just sitting around looking somber. He probably was having fun at these festivities.

If you believe Jesus was always serious, you have been given a wrong idea. He must have been a tremendous person to have around. When you think of all the men and women he attracted he would surely have had a wonderful sense of humor.

When you have a sense of humor and have a smile on your face you attract people to yourself. So, again our image of Jesus is distorted if we think he was only a serious and somber person.

The next point I want to make is that when we use Jesus to justify our anger, we have missed the whole message of Jesus. Jesus, in the Sermon on the Mount, and all the way through the Gospels, speaks about our anger.

He speaks about loving our enemies, doing good to those who hurt us, and doing good to those who persecute us. In that one scene in John's Gospel, where he drives out the buyers and sellers, it portrays Jesus as being angry.

People use this as an excuse and say I can be angry because Jesus was angry. What if I were to tell you that Jesus was not angry? As a teacher I can really address this. I was a vice principal for six years and it required that I be an actor.

There were times when I had to get the attention of six hundred boys. I had to behave in such a way they knew I was there and I had a message. And that they had better listen to what I had to say.

So I would act in a very dramatic way and I would say to them, "Now men, I am either a teddy bear or a polar bear. It's up to you which one I am going to be." Of course I was putting on an act.

Now Jesus was a teacher and there were a great many people around at the time of Passover when this incident happened in the temple area. There were probably thousands of Jews, because of the Passover they had to be there, and Jesus knew he had to get the attention by doing something dramatic.

I believe he was thinking... "I have a message to get across and if this is the only way I am going to attract your attention then this is the way it has to be." I do not see Jesus as angry.

Why? Just think about it. When you are angry you are attacking and you are at war with someone. When you are at war with someone, you cannot be at peace. You have given away your God-given peace to someone else and have said, "You have the power to change me from a nice gentle person into a raving maniac."

I believe Jesus never lost the peace of God. I believe that Jesus was always in a state of oneness with God. He was aware of that and therefore he was aware that he could not attack. How do you attack when you are at peace? Attack is only something you do when you are in a state of war.

> So you are either in a state of peace or you are in a state of war. You cannot be in both at the same time... Amen.

Jesus was being a very good teacher. He'd make a very good vice principal. And he did get his message across, didn't he? We cannot use this example to justify our anger because it is a distortion of who Jesus really is.

If we look at Jesus from a positive point of view, we see that he was a spiritual savior. Jesus came to free us from our sins and the effects of our sins. His overwhelming message was this: that our sins have no effect on God's love for us.

The sickness of scrupulosity is when we have the audacity, the arrogance, to think that our petty sins can change God's mind. Think about this...Here we have a God, who is happy as anything, but then we commit a sin and so God turns into a raving maniac.

Do you think we really have that kind of power? To think for one moment that we have the power to stop God from loving us is the height of arrogance. What we need is humility.

I believe Jesus came to say to us... Look you've made a lot of mistakes, you really blew it but it did not affect my love for you. There is no way you could change God's mind for when God created you he spoke and said, "you were good" and God is still saying it.

God has never stopped saying it. Jesus is telling

us that the separation between God and us has been mended, healed. Jesus is the mediator for he is the one who has come to stand between us and God and is telling us that we are OK.

We can go to Jesus with the assurance that He is the link, the bridge between ourselves and God. Jesus is the healer, not just of the body, but he heals any sense of separation or alienation we feel towards God. The message of Jesus is universal and I repeat, Jesus is the savior of all people. Everyone is free to go to him.

One of the beautiful things that I have seen, are pictures of Jesus as Black, or Chinese, or Japanese, or Mexican. I have seen pictures of him as Oriental, as Indian as well because that is what He is! Jesus is the savior of the whole world!

He is not just the savior of the white race. His message of peace is to be proclaimed to all the nations. Jesus is our model, the example of what it is to be created by a loving God.

When we reflect on Jesus we can say that is what God intended from the beginning. Jesus solves the mystery of God. Have you ever wondered who God is or what God is about?

All you have to do is look to Jesus and you will see the Father. He said it of himself. So if you want to know anything about God, go to Jesus because he is a chip off the old block.

Jesus is manifesting, or revealing the Father for us. The mystery of God has been revealed and solved in Jesus. Jesus is our personal savior. As a result of the Resurrection Jesus can span time and space. He can be everywhere at the same time.

The Eucharist is a beautiful example of this. No matter where you go, Jesus is present and you have his full attention. In his glorified and resurrected body, Jesus has no time barriers or space barriers.

Maryanne told me that at one time she used to come to chapel to make a holy hour every week on Wednesday. Most times the chapel would be empty and she'd be so happy to have the full attention of Jesus in the Blessed Sacrament.

When someone else would come in she would be upset and distracted because she felt Jesus attention was divided and she didn't have his full attention anymore. She laughs at it now.

Jesus is here for each and every one of us at any given time and space with his full, undivided, unconditional love. Jesus speaks to us today. He speaks to you, to me. He speaks in the Eucharist and what Jesus is saying is probably the most important message that we can ever hear.

*"I will never leave you. I will never abandon you. I am with you always now and forever."* Amen. Praise God.

## Sitting at the Feet of Jesus

### Father Peter McCall, OFM, Cap.
*(Transcribed from audio)*

Most of you are aware of my likeness for one-liners. So, I was greeted this afternoon with a couple of one-liners which may be extremely important for many of you. The first one says...Life is uncertain, so eat dessert first. We never know when something is going to happen so get that dessert in! The next one says... Things get better with age, so I am approaching magnificence.

What we are going to do, in this second part of the year, is to have a series on the wisdom of Jesus. What I would like you to do as we enter into the Mass, to cel-

ebrate the Presence of Jesus here, is to take on the mind
of a disciple. In other words have an open mind, the
mind of a truth seeker.

We are all students and teachers, one to another.
Let's have the attitude of just sitting at the feet of Jesus,
the Master teacher. He is the only one we can call Master because Jesus is the Messiah, our teacher and we
are his disciples.

September is the month when people return to school.
I would like to suggest that you take on the mind of a
student when we reach the proclamation of the Gospel
and the homily. This world is a classroom and we are
constantly learning.

I will speak a little more about time during the homily because one of the proverbs of Jesus, that we will
hear, is about time.

Many of us have a great deal of anxiety, problems
with time, because we see time as linear. We see there
is a past, we see there is a future, and sometimes we get
taken up with so much guilt of the past, or the anxiety
of the future that we miss the present moment.

It's in this present moment, right now, that is happening and we miss it. We are forever looking back or
looking ahead. Whereas healing and where God is, is
right here, right now.

God is in this present moment. If we have a student's
mind, the mind of a searcher, we will seek wisdom. We
will begin to express that wisdom in our hearts and in
our minds and that wisdom as we will see will heal us.

## A proclamation of the Gospel of Matthew

These are the words of Jesus, our Messiah, the master,
the teacher. Just allow these words to speak to you as
a Rhema. (A Rhema is a personal word to each of us individually and is derived from the Greek word, meaning
"inspired word.") Listen to the powerful words of wisdom

that come from the mouth of Jesus.

And Jesus said to the crowds, "Do not store up for yourselves treasures on earth where moths decay and destroy and thieves break in and steal. But store up treasures for yourself in heaven, where neither moth, nor decay destroys, nor thieves break in and steal.

"For where your treasure is, there also your heart will be. No one can serve two masters. You either hate one and love the other. Or be devoted to one and despise the other. You cannot serve God and money.

"Therefore, I tell you, do not worry about your life. What you are to eat or drink. Or about your body, what you are to wear. Is not life more important than food, and the body more important than clothing?

"Look at the birds of the air. They do not sow or reap. They gather nothing into barns. Yet your heavenly father feeds them. Are you not more important than they? Can any of you by worrying add a single moment to your life?

"Why are you anxious about clothes? Learn from the way the wild flowers grow. They do not work, they do not spin. But I tell you that not even Solomon in all his glory was arrayed as one of these.

"If God so clothes the grass of the field, which grows today and is thrown into the fire tomorrow, will he not much more provide for you, 0 you of little faith? So do not worry and say what are we to wear, or what are we to drink, or what are we to wear? All of these things, the pagans seek.

"Your heavenly Father knows that you need them all. Seek first the kingdom of God and his righteousness, and all these things will be given to you besides. Do not worry about tomorrow. Sufficient for the day is the evil thereof." This is the Gospel of the Lord.

I would just like to take a few of these proverbs of Jesus and see the wisdom that is behind them. Jesus tells us, "Do not store up treasures on earth where moths

decay or thieves break in and steal. For where your treasure is, there your heart will be found."

I found out that this beautiful proverb was significant
to our family. When my Aunt Dolly was about 75 years
old, she was moving from East Rockaway out to Arizona
where her son lived, and she wanted to visit the tomb of
her mother, which would be my great-grandmother, at a
cemetery in Brooklyn.

She asked my brother, Tom, who was a Jesuit and I
if we would go there with her to the tomb. We asked her,
"Well how are you going to find it?" And she said, "It's
very simple. It's the stone that says 'Where your heart
is, there your treasure will be'."

So it is written on the tomb of my great-grandmother.
What is so important about this phrase is that it tell us
what we value is what we seek. Jesus would have us
value those things which are important and let go of
those things that are not. We need to realize what our
priorities are.

Of course, we make value judgments all day long. I
recall my sister asking me, "Why don't you call me more
often?"

I would reply, "Well, I just don't have the time." And
you know something. That was a lie. Why? Because what
was actually happening was that I chose other things to
be more valuable than calling my sister. A value judgment is when we use our time in other ways. That's all.

What we have to do in order to be healed is to begin
to take responsibility for our value system. We are really
doing what we want to do, despite the fact that we say
we are not.

We say we would like to have more time to read, or to
meditate or whatever. The fact is you have it, you have
all the time in the world but what we do, we are doing it
because we value it.

I'm asking you to begin to understand that we need

to take responsibility for what we see as being important, including the idea of suffering. In our addictive society, and in our dysfunctional families, suffering was
often praised.

We were usually given models of people who endured
great pain and suffering. They are featured on the front
pages of magazines. Most of us have an investment in
suffering which we really don't understand.

However one of the reasons we get sick is because
there is value in that. We may get a lot of attention because of it. This is only a small example and of course
this is all unconscious, but we have to begin to realize
this is what we are doing. And we are making a value
judgment.

Now if we want to change, we need to change our values and once you change your values, your behavior will
follow. When we enter into the mid-life crisis, we find
we have pursued values that we thought that society
told us were important only to find out it wasn't working
anymore for us.

So we take stock and realize we have to change our
values as to what is important and what is not. St. Paul
writes, *"What I used to think as gain, I now consider rubbish." (Re: Phil. 3:8)*

Rubbish! That's a nice English word for a Greek four
letter word. Yes, he said what you think he said! When
Paul experienced Christ on his way to Damascus, his
whole value system was destroyed. He had to begin to
reconsider and change his way of thinking.

The next proverb is similar, where Jesus says, "no
one can serve two masters." We cannot serve the world
and the Holy Spirit. We are a house divided against itself. We are trying to do two things which are mutually
exclusive by trying to live the worldly way and the life of
the Spirit.

We just simply cannot do it because if Jesus is our

Master, we cannot also serve the ego. One will have to go. We cannot live in light and in darkness at the same time. We cannot serve life and death. We have to make a commitment to one and let the other go.

The reason many people are not healed is because of procrastination. Many people are just walking on the fence, trying to serve life and death, both the ego and the Spirit. In doing this juggling act, we are serving two gods and so there is tension. We can only serve one Master, either Jesus or the world, not both.

The next proverb of Jesus: *"do not worry about tomorrow...tomorrow will take care of itself. Sufficient for the day is its own trouble."* One would almost think that it was a slogan that came right out of the Twelve-Step program of Alcoholics Anonymous,

"One day at a time." In other words we have enough problems in the present moment. Why worry about the past or why be concerned about the future. It is in this present moment that is the important moment of healing. It is in this present moment that God is and healing takes place.

When I said I was going to speak about time, this is it. It is always what is going on right now. Anything else is, either 'what's so' or 'so what.' 'What's so' is what is happening right up to now, at this very moment. What has happened to you in the past is, 'so what.' What is important is 'what's so,' what am I doing right now? What am I feeling right now? What's the decision I'm making right now?

I said at the beginning of Mass, we have problems because we think life is linear or one dimensional.

I tend to think, there is a past and a future and I'm sort of stuck in this moment. Let us look at it in a simpler way. Instead of seeing time or life as linear, let us see life as circular.

This was the way our ancestors saw time before the

Industrial Revolution. It all began with the Industrial Revolution when they started putting clocks up on steeples and people had to be at work at seven a.m. Up until then, there was only three times a day, morning, noon and night. Life was simpler.

They would say to one another, "I'll see you in the morning." It could mean eight o'clock or eleven o'clock. Or they'd say I'll see you this afternoon or this evening. The afternoon could be anywhere between noon and five. After that it was nighttime.

The concept of time for them was a circular pattern because of the seasons and most people were farmers prior to the Industrial Revolution. They planted and reaped and the sun came up and the sun went down. And they started all over again. The seasons of the year always returned and life was repetitive and circular.

If you didn't get things all done one day, you'd get them done the next day. If you didn't learn your lessons today you'd learn your lessons the next day. There was no big deal and they had a beautiful concept of time.

They accepted the fact that people were born and that people die and life went around and around again. If we failed to learn something today we'll have an opportunity to learn it tomorrow. And it will keep coming around until we get it right.

This concept of time doesn't have the guilt about the past and the anxiety of the future. The belief was that time will take care of itself. It's a beautiful concept.

So, as disciples of Jesus we have been listening to the wisdom of Jesus. Let us take it into our hearts and minds.

Let us pray:
Heavenly Father, we thank you for your Son Jesus, for the Rabbi Jesus .our Master, our Guru, and the Messiah. We thank you for St. Matthew who recorded the wisdom of the

Sermon on the Mount.

May each of us understand that as your followers you would want us to be wise and discerning persons. Help us to demonstrate this wisdom in the way that we act and speak towards each other. Help us to perceive the world around us with the power of your wisdom.

In the name of the Father God, In the name of Jesus and through the power of the Holy Spirit, through the intercession of Mary, the mother of Jesus, we ask and pray for the gift of divine wisdom. Help us to be a wise people because we have a wise Savior and Messiah. Amen.

## The Healing Spirituality of the Twelve Step Program

I firmly believe that the Twelve Step Program of Alcoholics Anonymous was inspired by the Holy Spirit. Since 1939, this program has brought healing and recovery to over two million people around the world. No church can make that statement. God is definitely involved in this program and it has been truly a gift to so many sufferers who would never have experienced healing without it. I praise God for this wonderful gift to all of us.

The power of the Twelve Step Program is that it is extremely pragmatic on one hand, yet based on solid theoretical principles known by the spiritual masters for ages.

This power is seen in the fact that this program has been adapted to heal all sorts of compulsions and dependencies far beyond the expectations of those who originally formulated them.

In 1939, the word "co-dependent" did not even exist, much less the whole concept of co-dependency being a disease in itself. The scope of this program is amazing in how it has brought sobriety, sanity and sanctity to so many people.

The truth upon which this program is based is that addiction and dependency are spiritual problems and that only a spiritual program can heal them.

Carl Jung once said that all problems for people over forty years of age were spiritual. I think we can safely bring that age down quite a bit. So many of our problems are spiritual in nature, and the admission of this fact has opened the door to so much healing.

I am approaching the Twelve Steps as a Catholic priest involved in a healing prayer ministry within the framework of the Charismatic Renewal. My intention in this presentation is to use my background in charismatic spirituality and healing prayer and apply them to the Twelve Steps as I understand them.

What I will try to do is to expose the great spiritual truths on which the Twelve Steps are based, and share how the charismatic healing principles might apply to both dependency and co-dependency. I hope to explain why I think the program is so successful, and present Twelve Healing Truths which make this program such a powerful healing program.

First, I would like to give an overview of the Twelve Steps without going into any of them individually. They can be divided into three parts: Part one consists of the first two steps. Part two consists of steps three to nine. Part three consists of the final three steps.

Part one, the first three steps, is different from the other steps in that they do not demand that we do anything, but simply *"come to our senses."(Lk. 15:17)* The program does not really end with a "spiritual awakening," it begins with one.

The admission of personal powerlessness is the most profound and far-reaching moment of grace that we will ever experience. It is the first step on a spiritual path that radically changes our lives. This path leads out of the insanity of dependence on chemicals or relationships to the sanity of sobriety and sanctity.

It is an example of the great paradox that Jesus spoke about so often, the Pascal Mystery. *"Unless a grain of wheat falls into the ground and dies, it remains just a grain of wheat. But, if it dies, it produces much fruit."(Jn. 12:24)*

The Twelve Steps, as a spiritual path, begins with a moment of truth. *"You shall know the truth, and the truth will set you free." (Jn. 8:35)* This "teachable moment" is total grace, that is, not earned or deserved in any way.

Part two, steps three through nine, are very personal and make up the affirmative action which we are now willing to do because we prefer sobriety to insanity. Just as humility (honesty) was the basis for part one, obedience is the basis for part two.

The scripture which best summarizes part two is: *"So it is with faith; if it does not have works, it is dead." (Jms. 2:17)*

On one hand, faith may be total gift, (Re: Rom. 46) as we have seen in part one. But, those of us in the program know that without our participation, faith is dead.

It is interesting to note that the affirmative action prescribed in part two of the program is the traditional forms of conversion known through the ages: an examination of conscience, confession, contrition, forgiveness and reparation.

Some people come to the program expecting something new and sensational, something they never heard before. Yet, what we hear is what the spiritual masters have taught for centuries: be honest with yourself, admit your faults, forgive and make reparation for the past. There is nothing new in the Twelve Steps. The difference is that now it is a matter of our survival.

The Twelve Step Program is based on selfishness, in the best sense of the word. It is selfish in the sense that it is "self-caring." If we do not see ourselves as worthy to be healed for our own good, we will never do what the program demands.

We know from experience that any other motivation, no matter how noble it may be, simply does not work. Many people have sought healing because they want to take care of their children, or because they want to do something for God.

Yet, the survival rate among those who see their worth outside themselves (the perfect definition of code-pendent) is not very high. Jesus tells us that we are "... to love our neighbor as we love ourselves." (Mt. 22:39) Authentic self-love is necessary for this program to work. Without it, we will abandon the path.

Part three, steps ten to twelve, are the 'nuts and bolts" of the program. This part describes the necessary daily routine for survival.

There is no substitution for daily examination, prayer and meditation, and sharing what we have received from others. There is no magic to this program as there is no magic to authentic healing.

Healing is always a process. It takes the "labor pains" of daily persistence and perseverance to be healed. We tell people that it is simple to be healed, but it is not easy.

Those who "skip steps" or try to short-circuit the healing process, will come up empty. Healing is both gift and hard work.

What I will do now is list and comment on what I call the Twelve Healing Truths on which the Twelve Step Program is based. Because the program is based on truth, it works.

Although I will sometimes make the distinction between dependency and codependency, the principles of healing apply equally to both.

Only the forms (a substance or a relationship) are different. The content (the purpose) of both dependencies is the same.

1. <u>Healing is dying to the false-self</u>. What does this mean? Somewhere in our growing up we accepted as true beliefs and assumptions about ourselves that were totally false.

These false beliefs and assumptions make up what we call the "false-self." In the area of codependency, one of these beliefs is that we receive our worth and value in relationship with another person, or with our work and success.

Once we seek our worth outside ourselves, we put our happiness in the hands of another person and set ourselves up for failure. The failure that will inevitably happen is that the person or thing in which we placed our value will fail us or abandon us.

However, the pain of this failure now becomes our moment of truth. As Winston Churchill said when London was being bombed, "This is our finest hour." As our idols fail us, we are forced to confront the truth.

Jesus taught this many times. Unless we are humbled, we will never be exalted. Unless we become bankrupt, we will never seek another alternative. Unless we have a breakdown, we will never experience true life.

This moment has sometimes been called the "midlife crisis." Having functioned for over forty years under an illusion, suddenly our life falls apart. This has been compared to "climbing a ladder to the top, only to find out that you are against the wrong wall."

What went wrong? The truth now appears that we have been living a lie. We had been trying to make it on our own. We thought we were right. It is now apparent we were wrong.

What a beautiful moment of grace! Everyone should have a nervous breakdown. It is the best thing that can happen to us. Only then can we reach what the educators call a "teachable moment."

We will finally "take the cotton out of our ears and put it in our mouths." Just how far we have to go to "bottom out" is up to us. Some have to hit the pits, others seem to awaken before all is lost. Sooner or later we have to come to the realization that nothing outside ourselves can save us. We eventually have to *come to our senses.* (Re: Luke 15:17)

Is it true that some never face this truth? Obviously, the answer is "yes." All we have to do is look at the misery in so many families where addicts still cling to their own ideas and justify their destructive behavior. We are to learn from our suffering, not continue in it.


2.   <u>Healing is accepting a power beyond ourselves</u>. What does this mean? In a moment of grace we realize that there is a power within us that is not our own, but which can do for us what we could never do for ourselves.

This power in the program is called "Higher Power." Many of us thought we had a relationship with God, but the God we believed in was not the true God.

We had a codependent relationship with an idol that we made up. We manipulated and controlled this idol like we did with every other relationship in our lives. Just as we had a "love/hate" relationship with those around us, we have the same relationship with this idol we call God.

This is why so many who come to the program have a hard time beginning a spiritual path. They thought they were on one, but their idol failed them just as all their other relationships failed them.

The true God who saves us gets very bad press. This is seen in our insurance policies which insure us against an "act of God."

An act of God is a presumed disaster which has no apparent cause except God, a wrathful God who destroys what we build. This basic presumption shows how far away we are from understanding the nature of God.

No wonder we do not go to God to be healed; we believe it was God who afflicted us in the first place.

Finally, in a moment of truth, our illusions are exposed. We begin to be willing to believe in a Power for good that is within us and wants to help us. Slowly, but surely, we begin to trust this Power. To our surprise, it works.

This Power had always been on our side, but we did not realize it. Now we are willing to accept this power as "out to help us."

3. <u>Healing is accepting all as grace (gift).</u> What does this mean? It means that our belief that we have to earn our salvation has fallen apart. In a moment of spiritual awakening we realize that salvation is a free gift from God.

All of us who have been healed by this program know, beyond a shadow of a doubt, that we did not deserve it. This is a great truth. As dependents and co-dependents we used all sorts of control and manipulation to get what we wanted.

All of a sudden it dawns on us that we cannot manipulate God. How can we merit or earn what is freely given?

4. <u>Healing is faith in action.</u> This means that once we have acknowledged our personal powerlessness and come to the realization that only a power beyond our-

selves can heal us, we turn our will and life over to this Higher Power by listening and obeying.

This is the third step of the program. It has been said that the whole program is summed up by living out this step.

Someone once wrote, *"Let no one be deluded that knowledge of the path can substitute for putting one foot in front of the other."* Faith without works is dead. (Re: Jms. 2:17)

In many of the miracles of Jesus, we see that he asks the person to do something: *"Pick up your mat." (Mt. 9:6) "Stretch out your hand." (Mark 3:5)* Healing may be a gift, but we have to accept it by acting on it.

For co-dependents, this principle may not so much mean doing something as stop doing something. Stop making excuses for our partner's irresponsible behavior. Stop trying to be another's savior. Stop denying destructive behavior.

Co-dependency has been defined as a disease where two people agree to deny each other's faults. It is an unholy alliance where we sacrifice our own good for the destruction of another. To be healed, we have to stop being insane by letting other people make their own mistakes.

5. <u>Healing is accepting personal responsibility</u>. This means that healing begins where blame leaves off.

To see ourselves as victims or martyrs is a luxury that we can no longer afford. Martyrdom has been something that has been handed down to us as something good.

Actually, martyrdom in the early church had nothing to do with passively accepting something we had no control over. Martyrdom was an active participation in giving witness to one's faith in Jesus.

They were active witnesses to their faith. Somewhere

along the line the word came to mean a passive submission to evil. St. Paul tells us, *"Do not be conquered by evil, but conquer evil with good"* ( Rom. 12:21).

When we passively submit to evil, we are not giving witness to the power of God. The true meaning of "martyr" is a witness.

We are to testify to the power of God. Someone once said that evil increases because good people do nothing. The other thing about playing the role of martyr is that on an unconscious level, we deeply resent it and a lot of suppressed rage is going on within us.

There is nothing holy about this. This resentment eventually expresses itself in violence when we are not able to suppress it anymore. We see this often when so called good people just blow up in a violent rage and do some insane act.

This principle of accepting personal responsibility is seen in step four of the program where we are asked to take a searching and fearless personal inventory of our life.

We have to ask ourselves honestly, "Where have we become coconspirators with the forces of our own destruction? The purpose of the inventory is not to make us guiltier. We have enough guilt without adding more.

It is simply to expose those areas of our lives where we have participated in our own misery without justification or condemnation. In fact, the inventory is also intended to bring to our attention our strengths as well as our weaknesses.

Co-dependents find this step very difficult because dishonesty is so characteristic of the disease. Projecting blame and finding scapegoats for our misery is at the heart of co-dependency.

Co-dependents believe that others should make personal inventories. This whole program is based on honesty and without honesty it will never work. Healing demands an end to our "pity parties" and "guilt trips" and getting on with our participation in getting well again.

6. <u>Healing is non-rational.</u> This means that we do not have to fully understand what we are doing in order to do it. Someone once said, "Analysis leads to paralysis."

The greatest enemy to our healing is rationalization. We can rationalize ourselves right out of healing, no matter how much we say we want it. Rationalization leads to procrastination which is the way we prevent ourselves from being healed.

One of the reasons why the Twelve Steps is so successful is that it is so successful. Even the greatest procrastinator has to admit this.

People who have little faith in God and in a spiritual path have come to this program because it works. They do what they are told even though they do not understand all the reasons behind what they are doing. They have faith in the program. It works without explanations. The whole thing is non-rational, but it works.

Healing is non-rational in that it is not a result of left-brain reasoning, but right-brain insight and intuition. Higher Power will speak to us more by intuition than by reason.

Dependents find this very hard because they are masters in control. We stay in control when we use our left-brain. To have to depend on intuitions is seen as fearful. Yet, it is exactly in this risk that healing can be found.

7. <u>Healing is commitment to Life</u>. In the terminology of the program, this means that sobriety is to be our overwhelming priority.

Nothing is to be more important than maintaining our sanity. Everything in our lives is subject to our commitment to sobriety or freedom from addictive behaviors.

In our many years of being involved in a healing ministry, we see one characteristic which dominates those who were healed from those who were not.

That characteristic is that their "life urge" was greater than their "death wish." This commitment to life has nothing to do with fear of death.

Some people do stay alive because they are afraid of death. But, fear of death will never heal. It only prolongs misery. What we mean is a joy of living, a life-urge that overcomes any death-wish no matter how subtle it might be.

It would be helpful at this time to mention just how serious co-dependency is as a disease.

It looks good, but it kills. It should not be treated lightly. There is a subtle death-wish in this disease which, if not treated, will not kill a person right away, but makes for a miserable life before death. Statistics show that co-dependents will usually die before the dependents who they are trying to help

Healing is choosing those options which promote and encourage life. We know what we see as important when we look at our choices. We seek what is valuable to us. Jesus taught this in his parables of the "hidden treasure" and the "pearl of great price." (Mt. 13:44-50) We show by the decisions we make what we see as important. If it is really important to us to enjoy life, we will make healing decisions.


8. Healing is forgiveness. In the words of the program, this means "to let go and let God." Forgiveness is more willingness than being willful. It is a decision we make if we really want to be healed.

To choose not to forgive is a decision to remain unhealed. We choose to be right rather than happy. It is an established fact that we cannot be healed as long as the poison of unforgiveness is flowing through our bodies. It is a self-caring decision because we know that we cannot be healed without forgiveness.

Forgiveness has nothing to do with the people we see as hurting us. We "take them off the hook" whether they want to or not. We do not even have to go to them and tell them that we have forgiven them. In fact, there are times when we should not do this or perhaps circumstances will not allow us to do it.

It makes no difference. All we have to do is be willing to see differently through the mind of Christ. Be willing to see the world without an enemy.

If we are having a hard time with forgiveness, it is because we have overlooked the one person we have to forgive the most...ourselves! The basis for forgiveness is "temporary insanity."

It is the same reason why Jesus forgave on the cross when he said, *"Father, forgive them. They do not know what they are doing." (Lk. 23:34)* We do not condemn insane people. Addictions are a definite sign of insanity.

Another basis for forgiveness is that we are dealing with "co-sufferers." We begin to realize that we are all suffering from the same disease. If we can forgive ourselves on the grounds of insanity, so we can forgive everyone else.

Just as we did not know what we were doing, the same would hold for anyone else. In healing, forgiveness and healing are synonymous. We cannot have one without the other.


9. <u>Healing is re-pair-ation</u>. What does this mean? It means correction without punishment. We do not use the word "reparation" because this word has the connotation of punishment. Punishment has nothing to do

with repairing any harm done.

Our insane world somehow sees suffering as a way of making up for something. Actually, all it does is satisfy some people's masochistic or sadistic desire for revenge. It does not fix anything.

True "reparation," which heals, does not bring pain or suffering to anyone on any level. It brings correction on the level that the harm was done. Healing reparation is simply trying to complete some unfinished business, that is, doing or saying something today which should have been done or said in the past.

Making amends simply means trying to mend, to heal a wound or hurt that was done in the past by a present act of love.

The problem with making amends is that sometimes it can cause more hurt if it is done at an inappropriate time or manner. We are not healed by making problems for other people.

Making amends should not be used as a weapon to make other people feel worse. We must make amends for our own sake, not for the sake of the other. It can be done symbolically if the other person has died or is not open to the gesture. However we make amends, we should seek discernment before we do or say anything.

10. <u>Healing is a process</u>. Healing is not magic. Just as it took time to get sick, so it takes time to get well. The key here is always accepting the present moment as the only moment that healing can take place. As the program would say, "One day at a time."

Dependency and co-dependency are learned behaviors taught to us by an addictive society. Society wants us to be dependent, so we need to be de-programmed to be healed. This type of healing cannot take place too quickly.

It may be a "born again" experience, but birthing takes time.

Comparing healing to giving birth is a good example because it explains the pain in being healed. Jesus himself used the example of *"a woman in labor"* to explain redemptive suffering. (Re: Jn. 16:21)

Pain is not good in itself, but giving birth to a new life can be painful. Once we are healed, we will forget the pain because of the joy of new life.

11. <u>Healing is perseverance.</u> We never lose unless we quit. This means that healing demands a routine to which we must be persistent, not perfect. Co-dependents tend to be perfectionists, even when they want to be healed.

To think that we will never make a mistake in our healing process is another illusion coming from the disease itself. The fact is, we all fail, but we are to be persistent in picking ourselves up again.

This is the healing process of turning set-backs into come-backs; turning stumbling blocks into stepping stones. It is a "day by day" journey. Sometimes it gets sloppy. We will not do it perfectly. The big thing is that we do it with a sense of humor and perseverance.

12. <u>Healing is sharing what we have received</u>. This means that we cannot keep something unless we give it away. We cannot keep our sobriety and sanity unless we share it with others.

In the program, this is known as "twelve stepping." Again it is done for a very self-caring motivation, our own sobriety and sanity. We do not reach out to others to manipulate or change them. This is another definition of co-dependency. We help others because our own survival is at stake. It is love without a price tag.

The success of the Twelve Step Program is found in those people who have been healed through the program and who now want to share their healing with others. The same can be said for all healing. Healing is not a private gift.

We are not healed for ourselves alone. Our healing is to extend to all we come in contact with every day. This is the way we express our gratitude for what we have received.

May the peace and love and joy of the Lord Jesus Christ be with you now and forever. Amen.

## The Serenity Prayer

God grant us the Serenity to accept the things
we cannot change;
Courage to change the things we can
and Wisdom to know the difference.

Living one day at a time and accepting
hardships as the pathway to peace;
taking as he did, this sinful world as it is,
not as I would have it;
Trusting that God will make all things right if
I surrender to His will;
That I may be reasonably happy in this life and
supremely happy with God forever in the next.

Amen.

*Reinhold Niebuhr, 1943*

## Conclusion

The original idea for this book came about as a result of meeting Maura Shaw on a retreat I was giving in New York in 2004. She had been one of the editors on another publication that featured a story about the healing work I was involved in.

I felt at that time that I had much to offer from my many years of experience in a healing prayer ministry and wanted to share it with others who would be interested. I had no idea how to go about it because any writing that I had done in the past had been in collaboration with Father Peter McCall and a team of people.

We coauthored and published through the House of Peace, Inc. three books on healing prayer. His death in 2001 placed me in a limbo state not knowing where I belonged. Very few understood the devastation and suffering I felt in losing him.

Maura encouraged me to start writing from my experiences and offered to help me even though she lived in New York and I had moved to Florida.

How do I start I wondered? Maura had outlined a number of subjects that were of interest to her after she had read my other three books and so I had that to begin with.

I must admit my heart was not in this work at first.

I was too distracted with computer glitches and became frustrated in trying to get it right. However once I began to write I realized what an important work this was.

It had taken me many years to bring about balance in my own life as a result of trying to follow the will of Jesus and The Holy Spirit. I was told by some pretty knowledgeable people on the subject of mental health that I must have been gifted with an enormous grace to be as well balanced and real as I have become despite the tumultuous events of my life.

I totally agreed with them, because at some point early on, I knew my life was unmanageable, that I was powerless and needed a saving grace. I desperately wanted to be healed of the emotional pain that was keeping me back from experiencing a full life.

At a time when I cried out for help, Jesus, my Lord and Savior, came to help me in ways that can only be described as mystery. I have come to believe that the reality of true spiritual enlightenment will ultimately save humankind and is basically the tenet of this book.

"Thank God for God" is one of my personal slogans. However it is directed toward the God of truth, the God of justice, The God of perfect unconditional love and overflowing joy.

Jesus Christ, Son of the Living God, who came to this earth plane so that we might be set free is the One I wanted to portray in this book. Jesus came to bring us, "The peace that passes all understanding." It is through the art and discipline of listening to that "still inner voice" that he speaks to us if we are but willing to have "ears to hear."

Eventually we will come to realize we were mistaken in believing what we were taught about God by other people. We can have access to a direct knowledge of God's love that is beyond anything we will ever understand or know.

We are able to experience for ourselves the "truth that will set us free." This love frees us from the bondages of darkness, negativity and self-doubt. This love transforms and renews our minds by guiding us towards a higher level of goodness, beauty, sweetness and purity.

Our minds become transformed and we behold the glorious light of the kingdom of God within.

We can in each and every moment, experience the Presence of Christ in our ordinary and extraordinary lives. Broken lives and hearts will be made whole again.

I pray that each person who reads this book falls in love with our God and Our Lord and Savior, Jesus the Christ, who has fallen in love with us from the moment of creation.

We are in reality never separated from the Presence of God. The belief that we are separated and apart is a falsehood. When we are tempted by wrongdoing; then is the time when we must turn to the Christ within who is always there waiting for us to return to our senses.

The living, loving Son of God, Jesus Christ, and the Holy Spirit who is within our minds will never abandon us as long as we recognize we are in need of right direction and guidance.

Whenever we need the answers to the questions that arise in our daily lives all we need do is look to the divine wisdom within and it will be revealed in whatever way is best.

*"Seek first the kingdom of God and all these things will be added to you." (Lk. 12:32)*

This book is about learning to be consciously united with God, the source of our existence and knowing that God's healing love is always in the heart of the Divine Presence.

Our work is to rest in God. When we relax, God's glory can shine in our life. This life does not belong to us. This life of ours belongs to God. We rest in the Divine

Presence and learn how to be peaceful and quiet. God is with us now and always.

Let us pray:
Loving Lord God I pray that as each person reads this book they will be given new hope and insights as to the unlimited possibilities that await them by turning their lives and wills over to the care of your eternal love. Amen.

I ask that each person be blessed with the awareness of your holy presence in their daily lives and they be granted the healing that is available through experiencing your loving kindness. I pray they be healed from the effects of abuse, grief, and destructive thoughts. May each person come to realize how precious they are as they bask in the sunshine of your loving Presence. I pray that your Love will fill every atom of their being and they will be transformed in body, mind and spirit. May they grow in the awareness of the Divine life within them and may it increase daily.

I offer The Holy Spirit my sincere gratitude and devotion for all the countless healings I have received throughout these many years. I praise and adore you now and forever. In the holy and glorious name of our Lord and Savior, Jesus Christ, I pray. Amen and Amen.

A Personal Testimony
James Gannon

Like so many others, I have received many, many gifts through the teachings and healing work of Maryanne Lacy and Father Peter McCall. I truly believe these gifts are so bountiful because they actually come directly from God through the work of this blessed ministry.

It is easy, (and accurate) to say that all things come from God. But to easily focus on this fact without proper appreciation for the ways God has chosen to work and those through whom He has chosen to work, deprives us of perhaps the most potent and efficacious healing attitude we can exercise the attitude of gratitude. Of the many gifts I have received, the opportunity to share in this testimonial is one that I will treasure most highly.

I attended my first, "First Saturday" healing Mass at Blessed Sacrament Monastery in Yonkers, New York in 1990 when I was 24 years old. I was in perfect health. Or so any doctor would have told me. That is mainly because sadness, despair, loneliness, isolation, fear and shame are only identifiable medical conditions in terms of the labels that are used to group and categorize them.

While sometimes medications are prescribed to

make the path bearable, the true path to find joy, hope, intimacy, community, courage and love have yet to be packed in a readily consumable form. So, these are left for us to find "on our own."

Of course we are not truly on our own. We merely have to accept responsibility for participating in our healing. I remember Father Peter say that the title of the book he and Maryanne wrote, "Rise and be Healed," was an admonition for us to take the steps we need to in order to show God that we are ready to do our part in the healing process.

I say now the single most important event in my road to recovering my relationship with God, and therefore my well-being, was my attendance at that first healing Mass.

Up to that point my life was, simply put, unmanageable. I now know, through what I learned from Father Peter and Maryanne, that my life was unmanageable because I was trying to do God's job for Him and ignoring the responsibilities that were mine. We all have some degree of unmanageability in our lives. It is a characteristic we must partially accept as part of our "humanness."

However this is not the kind of unmanageability of which I now speak. I'm addressing the pain of severe isolation and loneliness, deep shame coupled with a paradoxical grandiosity, feelings of persecution, obsession with self, profound anger and despair–and of course, the circumstances of our lies accompanying these spiritual illnesses: disease, debt, and distressed or broken relationships.

The work of Father Peter and Maryanne helped me find the cure. Now, to those familiar with their work, and twelve-step healing spirituality, this is going to sound like the "First Step", admitting to being powerless and that our lives have become unmanageable.

I heard Father Peter on many occasions speak of the twelve-step healing spirituality, as initially developed by Alcoholics Anonymous, as one of the most healing doctrines of our time. For those of us that are Christians, we see and hear something underlying the gift of the twelve-step healing tradition, the love, wisdom and eternal presence of our Savior and redeemer, Jesus Christ. The saying, "Give a man a fish, feed him for a day. Teach a man to fish, feed him for life," is especially pertinent here, considering the fish is one of the symbols of Jesus. Those of us blessed to have benefited from the work of Father Peter and Maryanne have, in a sense, been taught to fish, and now have ready access to Jesus.

At that first healing Mass I attended, it probably took me about sixty seconds to begin sobbing deeply. I did not stop until I got back on the train back to Manhattan. It was the first time, (although I did not realize it at the time) that I was blessed for – and through my mourning. It was only the beginning.

As the Mass progressed, the healing and laying on of hands began. I witnessed another sign of the divine work that was being done through this Ministry. In the several weeks before I attended, I had become aware of the faultiness of my thought process.

This may be hard to understand for those who have not had a similar feeling about their own mental faculties. The best I can explain is to quote a common slogan used in the twelve-step program: "My best thinking got me here." Those who have "hit the bottom" and had a spiritual awakening realize that their thought process was an integral part of their maladaptive behavior patterns that contributed to the unmanageability and wreckage of their lives.

I will say, at the risk of being my old grandiose self, I did not know a more cerebral person than myself. My "thoughts" were everything. They were my friends, com-

panions, my defense and my consolation. I was reasonably well educated. I had studied and excelled at theology and philosophy with Jesuit professors at Fordham
University. I had surrounded myself with a highly cerebral and intellectual group of friends with Ivy League
educations and strong promise of social prominence in
the future.

I was highly involved in a community of artists in
various disciplines. In spite of all this I was a miserable wreck. Well, I did see I had problems. But what was
the solution? How could I actually change my thought
process? How could anything be done without thinking
about it first? And if I thought about it, well...wasn't that
the problem?

Maryanne came to the podium after Father Peter
concluded the Mass and began to pray in tongues. I still
feel like I should call it singing in tongues because it
seems to me that's what she actually does.

I have not heard Maryanne speak specifically of the
process of how she receives her intuitions from the Holy
Spirit when praying in tongues, but those of us blessed
to have been present at these Masses know of her gift for
being able to call those in the most immediate of prayer
and healing. While everyone would be invited to receive
prayers and the laying on of hands, this portion was for
those whose illnesses required recognition.

I had made up my mind that since, well, I wasn't really sick, that I would not have hands laid on me – that
I would just stay and pray. That decision changed when
Maryanne called that "someone" was having trouble
with their thought process.

If there was any skepticism I carried about the gifts
of Maryanne and Father Peter, it left that instant. One
would expect to hear those with acute physical ailments
called out at a Mass such as this, but someone having
trouble with their thought process? I have never spoken

to Maryanne about this, and perhaps she commonly receives intuitions about people's thought processes, but I went to every first Saturday healing Mass for the next four years and do not recall her specifically calling on someone that was having trouble with their thinking process.

The "healing" I experienced was not a linear process. It's not really a case of having suffered from something, experiencing the Holy Spirit through the healing masses and then having some type of recovery. I recall one of Father Peter's homilies about "stinking thinking" and holding onto grievances. I was (and on some days still am) subject to these things.

What caused me great pain and struggle in my early life was the disparity in the ways I felt guided and the way in which I experienced and perceived life. Father Peter taught me that God does not test us. That being said, I felt very much alone. And it hurt. A lot! Even when I went to regular Mass I so often could not reconcile what I heard the priest say to what I believed.

So much of what it seemed to me the church taught was very much at odds with what I believed to be God's love and will. I wanted to experience God and Jesus in new ways but felt tied by guilt and shame to more orthodox views.

I cannot over-emphasize the amount of emotional pain I was in and did not see any way out of it. It was rooted in a combination of early life experiences as well as the disparity between my truest convictions and accepted traditions.

This was when I was introduced to the healing Masses of Father Peter and Maryanne and their teams known as the Peace of Christ Prayer Ministry. Father Peter validated for me in his teachings what I had always intuited via an inner voice. His words were the first exterior confirmation of truths I had known since my earliest memories. The connection was, at times, startling. Let me share an example.

I have always been a highly prayerful and meditative person and can enter into deep prayer and meditation for long periods of time. The prayer through which I have most deeply connected to Jesus is the "Our Father." Once I was praying and meditating on the Our Father when I had one of my connective moments which started with the initial insight that our lives are actually prayers.

I realized then, that when Jesus responded to the disciples' request to be taught to pray, he did not merely give humanity a prayer. He gave us a model for how to live life. I was then "taught" how the Our Father was actually a "model" for daily living and I began to deconstruct it and meditate on it. It had all the feeling of one of those "ah-ha!" moments and it brought me a tremendous amount of peace.

At the next first Saturday healing Mass I attended, Father Peter's homily was about how the Our Father was a "paradigm" for daily living. His homily taught exactly what I had learned when I opened up to one of the inner truths of the Lord's Prayer. Father Peter's teachings and my inner voice were in unison.

I asked Father Peter if he would hear my confession. We are as sick as our secrets and I wanted to be healed. I also knew that there were no secrets from the Source of the voice I heard in Father Peter and that I would only be healed through and earnest desire to be honest. After confession Father Peter and I spoke concerning my need for his insight with regard to my spiritual path. I felt after that there was a profound bond with him.

For me, transcribing Father Peter's homilies is merely carrying on his work. I say 'merely' because it is not work for me in any way. Sometimes I have to make myself transcribe when I am tired and not in the mood or after a long day at work, but this does not mean it is "work."

I am a member of a prayer and meditation group that practices spiritual healing and has had the blessing of witnessing many wonderful miracles. I am blessed to have a peer group of people dedicated to God's will and living Christ centered lives. Group meditation and discussion are a big part of our group work and when I use the teachings of Father Peter and Maryanne to elucidate or create context for some of our principles it is so uplifting to see the smiles and light in people's eyes. It is the light of the Holy Spirit.

The words of Maryanne and Father Peter now comprise a large part of both my conscious and unconscious thought process. In moments of doubt, loneliness, fear or anxiety I will invariably recall their words and I am led to serenity. In a sermon by Father Peter that I recently transcribed, he said, "Serenity is the Kingdom of God on earth." The Holy Spirit was calling on me to accept healing and I have learned to do my best to be ever grateful to God in all the ways He eternally chooses to reveal Himself.

I want to express special gratitude in this testimonial to his special workers, Maryanne Lacy and Father Peter McCall and all the members of their ministry. To Maryanne, I want to say your love and prayers are greatly appreciated and felt and it is a blessing beyond words to be able to tell you all that you've done for me without knowing it.

Love,
James Gannon
New York, New York
Feb. 4, 2007

Maryanne graduated in 1982 from the Archdiocese of New York training programs in Spiritual Direction and Religious Counseling. She has had further training in spiritual development and the spiritual exercises of St. Ignatius through the Center for Spirituality and Justice in the Bronx, NY. She is a long time member of the Association of Christian Therapists and was the leader of the St. Matthew's Prayer Group in Hastings-on-Hudson, NY from 1978-1982.

She first manifested the gift of healing in 1976 when she was praying over a woman who had a growth in her throat. The woman was healed instantly. Soon after, friends suggested that she meet Fr. Peter McCall, OFM Cap, who also had the gift of healing. For the next twenty-plus years they worked together as a healing team until Father McCall died in March 2001.

Father Peter and Maryanne had been praying for healing as a team since 1978 when they were asked to pray for a young man contemplating suicide, and his suicidal tendencies disappeared. From this first request came another from Maryanne's parish. This time a young woman was healed of Hodgkin's disease. Before long, many requests began coming in for their prayers. They celebrated their first Healing Mass at Mercy College Chapel, Dobbs Ferry, NY, on the feast of the Sacred Heart, June 1979.

Together they conducted workshops, gave retreats, and spoke at conferences all over the country. They had led healing pilgrimages to the Holy Land, France, Spain, Ireland, Italy and Canada. Both Father Peter and Maryanne have been members of the Association of Christian Therapists (ACT) since 1979. ACT is a professional organization of physicians, nurses and psychotherapists, who believe in and practice the healing power of prayer. They have been featured on local, cable and national television talk and news programs including "48 Hours," on CBS and a CNN special on healing prayer.

On August 24, 1981, they founded the Peace of Christ Prayer Ministry. They began with a healing prayer center at Blessed Sacrament Monastery, Yonkers, NY, which they named the House of Peace. It did not take long to outgrow that facility. On June 5, 1988, they moved to a more efficient office at 1291 Allerton Avenue, Bronx, NY

They have coauthored three books dealing with spiritual, emotional and physical healing: *An Invitation to Healing, Rise and Be Healed, What is Healing Prayer All About? Answers To Most Frequently Asked Questions About Healing.* Father Peter had recorded his teachings and had written many pamphlets distributed by the House of Peace. Maryanne has also recorded eight meditations.

In 2003 Maryanne was featured in the book *White Fire* by Malka Drucker

Maryanne is a Catholic laywoman – the mother of five children and grandmother of five. Maryanne relocated from Westchester County, NY, to Florida, which had always been her favorite vacation site.